The Heath
Guide to
Writing the
Research Paper

Gerald P. Mulderig
DePaul University

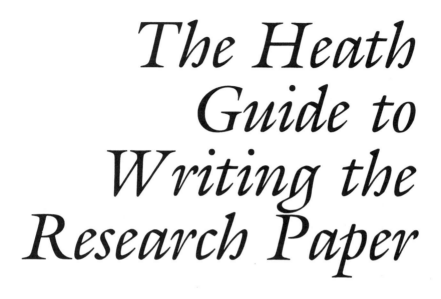

The Heath Guide to Writing the Research Paper

D. C. Heath and Company
Lexington, Massachusetts   Toronto

Address editorial correspondence to:

D. C. Heath and Company
125 Spring Street
Lexington, MA 02173

Published simultaneously in Canada.

Printed in the United States of America.

International Standard Book Number: 0–669–27704–5

10 9 8 7 6 5 4 3 2

Preface

This book serves as a guide and reference tool for both the novice and the advanced writer. Students new to research writing will find direction and assistance here as they move through each stage of the research process—defining a subject, discovering and evaluating potential sources of information, compiling a bibliography, taking notes, organizing and writing drafts, accurately citing sources, and professionally formatting the finished paper. Writers already experienced in doing research will appreciate the book's annotated lists of reference works, periodical indexes, and data bases, and they will find its presentation of MLA, APA, and endnote documentation clear, complete, and easy to use.

Originally published in a slightly different form as part of *The Heath Handbook,* Twelfth Edition, *The Heath Guide to Writing the Research Paper* combines the advantages of compactness with greater comprehensiveness than its size might at first suggest. Its features include the following:

1. An up-to-date presentation of library technology.

In addition to a thorough discussion of the traditional tools for research (including standard reference works, general and specialized periodical indexes, and government documents), Chapter 2 includes notes on finding materials with an on-line card catalog, explains how to use on-line data bases, and illustrates the kind of search made possible by CD-ROM technology. Annotated lists of important on-line data bases and CD-ROM data bases are also included.

2. **A complete guide to writing citations in MLA style, APA style, and traditional endnote style.**

Sections 3b, 6b, and 7b feature comprehensive and easy-to-use guides to writing citations in three of the most widely used styles of documentation. Nearly one hundred sample entries illustrate MLA and endnote citations for every kind of source that a student is likely to encounter, including government documents, interviews, films, lectures, recordings, television programs, and videotapes. Another thirty-nine sample citations provide equally complete coverage of APA documentation style. Convenient tables preceding each set of sample citations (see pages 39–41, 113–14, and 163–64) help students quickly locate the citation models they need, and extensive annotations explain the sometimes confusing rules for composing formally accurate citations.

3. **A clear and well-illustrated explanation of plagiarism.**

Section 4b examines both the accurate and inaccurate use of quotations and the differences between acceptable and unacceptable paraphrasing. Clearly annotated examples help students master these distinctions, and a handy two-step test aids them in determining when they must cite the source of material used in a paper.

4. **Practical advice on documenting sources with parenthetical citations.**

To help students document sources with professional attention to form, Sections 4c and 6c thoroughly explain the use of parenthetical citations in MLA and APA documentation. Both discussions illustrate the variations among parenthetical citation forms for such sources as anonymous works, multivolume works, works by two or more authors, and multiple works by a single author. They also suggest strategies for smoothly incorporating quoted and paraphrased material into one's own writing.

5. **Three sample student papers, illustrating MLA, APA, and endnote documentation.**

The three complete student papers in Chapters 5, 6, and 7 offer models for organizing and documenting research papers in MLA, APA, and endnote style. Extensive facing-page commentary not only provides helpful notes on matters of format, but also highlights the structure and development of these papers and examines the student writers' use of sources in composing them.

This project would not have been possible without the support and assistance that I received from many people at D. C. Heath and Company. To my editors—Paul Smith, Linda Bieze, and Karen Wise— go my special thanks for the time and talent that they committed to making this book a reality.

G. P. M.

Contents

1 The Research Process 1

   1a Thinking about your assignment 2
     1. The informative report 2
     2. The researched argument 4
     3. Shared features 6

   1b Thinking about a subject 7
     1. Be genuinely interested in your subject 7
     2. Be willing to search for a good subject 8
     3. Be prepared to make changes in your subject 8

   1c Thinking about your reader 9
   1d Planning the long paper 10
     1. Leave enough time 10
     2. Understand the research process 11
     3. Be prepared for the recursiveness of the research process 12

2 The Library 13

   2a The card catalog 13
     1. Reading catalog cards 14
     2. Locating books 15
     3. Using an on-line catalog 15

   2b Standard reference works 16
   2c Indexes to periodicals 24
   2d A special index: the *Essay and General Literature Index* 28

2e Data-base searches   29
    1. On-line searches   29
    2. CD-ROM searches   31
2f Government documents   34

3 Working with Sources   37

3a The working bibliography   37
    1. Assembling a working bibliography   38
    2. Recording bibliographic
       information   38
3b MLA Works Cited forms   39
3c Taking notes   55
    1. Note cards   55
    2. Types of notes   56
    3. Recognizing a potential "note"   59
3d Assessing your sources   60
    1. How current?   60
    2. How authoritative?   60
    3. How objective?   61
3e Assessing your subject   61
    1. Signs of a good subject   61
    2. Signs of a poor subject   61

4 Composing the
       Research Paper   68

4a Organizing and writing a research
    paper   68
    1. Know when to stop taking notes   69
    2. Organize your notes   70
    3. Compose a tentative outline   71
    4. Segment your writing   71
    5. Leave time for rethinking and
       revising   72

4b Avoiding plagiarism   72
    1. Quoting accurately   73
    2. Paraphrasing accurately   75
4c Citing sources   77
    1. Quotations   79
    2. Paraphrases   84
    3. Content notes   86
4d Formatting the research paper   87
    1. Paper   88
    2. Spacing and margins   88
    3. Title page   88

5 Student Research Paper A: MLA Documentation   93

6 Student Research Paper B: APA Documentation   112

6a Using APA documentation   112
6b APA reference list forms   113
6c Citing sources in APA style   125
    1. Quotations   126
    2. Paraphrases   131
6d Formatting a paper in APA style   132
    1. Paper   132
    2. Spacing and margins   133
    3. Title page   133
    4. Abstract page   134
    5. Text pages   134
    6. References page   134
    7. Footnotes page   134
6e Sample student paper   135

7   Student Research Paper C: Endnote Documentation   160

7a Using endnotes   160
　　1. Features of endnotes   161
　　2. Features of the endnote page   161
7b Endnote forms   162
7c Sample student paper   172

8   Mechanics   194

8a Manuscript preparation   194
　　1. Format   194
　　2. Quotations   195
　　3. Manuscript corrections   197
8b Capital letters   197
　　1. Proper nouns   198
　　2. Titles of works   200
　　3. Sentences and quotations   200
8c Numbers   201
8d Abbreviations   203
8e Italics   205
8f Syllabication   207

*The Heath
Guide to
Writing the
Research Paper*

The
Research
Process

When we open a newspaper at the end of a busy day, we may not think that we are doing research, but we are. We are doing research as we scan the paper for reports about the mayor's latest conflict with the city council, or about the response of the stock market to the Federal Reserve Board's new monetary policy. We are doing research when we copy a recipe out of the food section, check the standings of our favorite team, read a movie review, or hunt through the classified ads for a good used lawn mower. Research is part of the texture of our lives. It answers one of our deepest needs as thinking human beings—our need for information.

Gathering information is not a mechanical task; on the contrary, it constantly calls forth our powers of judgment and evaluation. After we have seen a baseball game or a new movie, we seek out friends to discuss it with, newspaper accounts or reviews to read. Why? By considering the opinions of people around us, we come to understand our own judgments better. Which play was really the turning point in the game? Which actor's performance was central to the film's success? We question and rethink our ideas not only during a debate in a noisy cafeteria or a crowded bar, but also in our silent interaction with the printed opinions of others.

The urge to do research, then, is rooted not simply in our curiosity but in our desire to understand. Behind every fact that engages our attention lies our natural wish to comprehend its meaning, our impulse to fit it into a context or pattern. Writing papers based on research satisfies that impulse, but it does something more: through the process

1

of gathering and evaluating information, it calls the writer into a kind of conversation with researchers who have preceded him or her. A research paper assignment is thus an invitation to become part of a far-flung community of thoughtful men and women, sharing their concerns, agreeing and disagreeing with their opinions, reflecting and expanding upon their conclusions.

1a Thinking about your assignment

The starting point in planning a research project is understanding what your instructor wishes you to do. Let's begin, therefore, by distinguishing between two different kinds of research papers, the **informative report** and the **researched argument**.

1. The informative report

The first type of research project, the informative report, attempts to describe, explain, or shed new light on a specific aspect of a subject. The writer of an informative report asks a question about this subject—a question, perhaps, that is somehow different from those that other people have asked—and answers it by collecting facts and viewpoints from various sources, by selecting out what seems to be particularly significant or interesting, and by assimilating this information into a paper that focuses and presents it in an original way. The informative report is never a mere summary of what someone else has said. Instead, it strongly bears the stamp of the researcher, both in the assertion that he or she makes about the subject and in the evidence that he or she chooses to support that assertion.

You will find an example of such a paper—Emmet Geary's "Recovery from the Florence Flood: A Masterpiece of Restoration"—in Chapter **7**. In this case the writer's assignment was to research any event from the 1960s and develop a paper that explored some specific aspect of that event. Like all researchers, Emmet began with a large subject—natural disasters—and only slowly zeroed in on a precise and manageable subject for investigation. The diagram on page 3 shows the stages by which he narrowed his subject.

Browsing among entries in the volumes of the *Readers' Guide to Periodical Literature* that span the 1960s (see **2c**), Emmet first moved from "disasters" to the narrower subject of "floods." One of the most

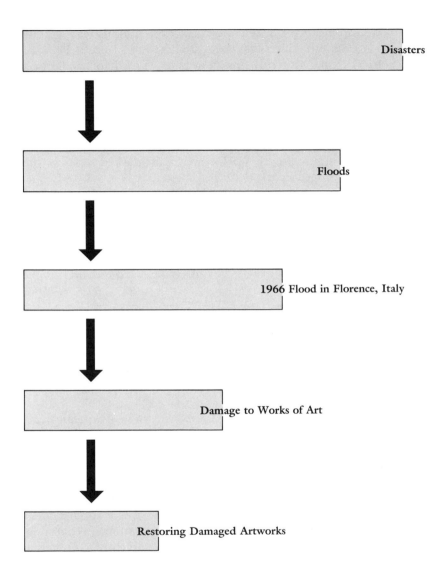

Emmet Focuses a Subject for Research

destructive floods of the decade, he learned through his reading, was the flood of the Arno River that devastated the Italian city of Florence in 1966. Realizing that this subject was too broad to handle in a comprehensive or original way, Emmet posed a question about it: Was any aspect of this flood unusual? What caught his attention as he read articles about the flood were reports about the damage done to Florence's unique collection of art treasures from the Renaissance. But even this subject, he discovered with further reading, could be focused into a still narrower one for his paper: the *restoration* of the works of art damaged by the flood.

Having arrived at this narrow subject, Emmet could now continue his research more efficiently, looking only for sources that dealt specifically with this topic and taking notes with a new sense of purpose and direction. The ultimate result was his tightly organized paper, which focuses on the unusual steps taken by professional restorers and concerned volunteers to save Florence's damaged treasures.

2. The researched argument

The second type of research paper uses evidence to shape an original argument. Rather than collecting and assembling materials to describe or explain a subject, the researcher who is writing an argument uses his or her research first to arrive at a judgment and then to defend that judgment before a reader.

The research papers reprinted in Chapters **5** and **6**—Suzanne Conlon's "Anne Bradstreet's Homespun Cloth: The First American Poems" and Cyndi Lopardo's "Career versus Motherhood: The Debate over Education for Women at the Turn of the Century"—are examples of this second type of paper. Cyndi wanted to write about women and education, but beyond those ideas she had not defined a subject. Like Emmet, she began by reading broadly in search of a specific topic that would interest her. An article on the history of women's education in *The Encyclopedia of Education* (see **2b**) aroused her interest in American higher education at the end of the nineteenth century, and particularly in the debate then raging over the appropriateness of rigorous academic programs for women. A bibliography at the end of the encyclopedia article sent Cyndi to two book-length histories of women's education in America, Thomas Woody's *A History of Women's Education in*

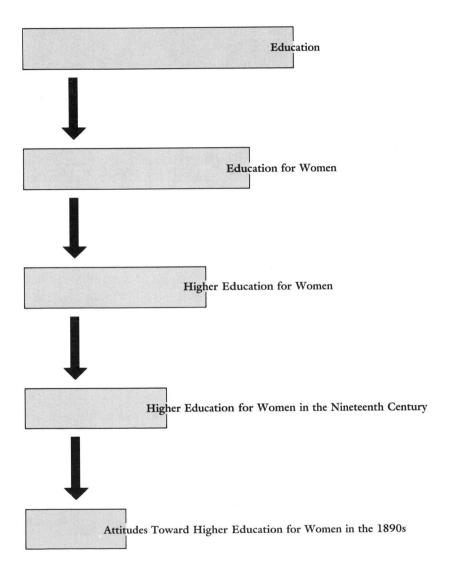

Education

Education for Women

Higher Education for Women

Higher Education for Women in the Nineteenth Century

Attitudes Toward Higher Education for Women in the 1890s

Cyndi Focuses a Subject for Research

the United States and Mabel Newcomer's *A Century of Higher Education for Women.*

Armed with the background information she acquired from reading the relevant portions of these two books, Cyndi next turned to the *Nineteenth Century Readers' Guide* (see **2c**) in search of a list of articles from the 1890s on the subject. Based on the articles she located there, she drew her own conclusions about the debate over higher education for women and tentatively formulated the argument she would present in her paper: that despite the increasing educational opportunities for women at the turn of the nineteenth century, much of society continued to regard higher education for women primarily as a means of enhancing roles within the home and family.

3.   Shared features

This summary of Emmet's and Cyndi's research procedures has oversimplified the often slow and complicated process of identifying a workable subject, but it illustrates two features that are common to both the informative report and the researched argument.

A research paper makes an assertion

First, a good research paper is focused around a central assertion. You needn't panic if, as you start your research, you're not sure what your paper's central assertion is going to be, for the fact is that it's impossible to know what assertion you can make about a subject until you have done a considerable amount of reading. As you acquire more and more information, though, you should begin to formulate *possible* assertions for your paper. After each session of researching your subject, ask yourself the following questions:

1. What am I *now* able to assert about my subject?
2. What do I think I *might* be able to assert about my subject with further research?

Use the answers to these questions to assess your progress and to direct your next research efforts. The final assertion that you make about your subject—the assertion that unifies your paper—will take the form of a thesis statement, a sentence that states your subject and indicates the specific point you wish to make about it.

A research paper reflects its writer's originality

The second feature common to both the informative report and the researched argument is originality. You may think there is little room for your own originality as a writer in a paper that is based on what other people have written about a subject, but that isn't true. Every good research paper owes its success to the researcher's unique talents as a thinker and investigator. The more creatively you have thought about your subject, the more distinctive your paper's focus will be. The more thoroughly you have researched your subject, the more diverse the sources of information that your paper will bring together. In its final form, your research paper will gather and present information about your subject in a way not duplicated by anyone else who has written on it.

1b   Thinking about a subject

If doing research is new to you, your first impulse may be to choose a topic that you already know well. Such a choice, however, is almost certain to rob your research of any interest or satisfaction, leaving you only with tedious and meaningless busywork. The purpose of research, after all, is not to document what you already know, but to discover what you do not know. As disturbing as it may sound at first, you are doing real research only if you do not know where it will lead.

1. Be genuinely interested in your subject

The fundamental requirement for a topic to research is the same as that which should guide the choice of any subject for writing: your true interest in it. In a freshman writing course, your instructor may leave the subject for your research paper entirely up to you, or may allow you to choose from a list of subjects or a general subject area. Even if your instructor limits the range of subjects more narrowly, you should seek out a specific angle or focus that for some reason appeals to you. Research is a process of discovery. You can participate in this process fully only if you select a subject that is a genuine question for you—a problem, a mystery, a tantalizing unknown quantity.

2.   Be willing to search for a good subject

You may have been able to find a good subject for the other papers you have written in freshman composition by turning to your personal experiences, your reading, or your entries in a journal. That will not be the case for a research paper. You will not be able to define a workable subject by sitting quietly at your desk and thinking deeply about the assignment. Instead, as our descriptions above of Emmet's and Cyndi's research procedures suggested, the process of identifying a potentially good subject for research begins with serious work in the library.

Although they were writing different kinds of papers, both Emmet and Cyndi began their hunt for a good subject in the same way: by looking for ideas and inspiration first in general sources of information. Emmet, searching for a topic from the 1960s, browsed through articles in the *Readers' Guide* until something in the titles he read attracted his attention. He did not complete the process of narrowing his subject—from disasters, to floods, to Florence, to the destruction of artworks, to the restoration of those works—in a single session in the library; instead, that process extended over several days of reading articles and thinking about them.

Cyndi, too, started with general reading—in her case, an encyclopedia in the field of education. When the topic of women's education in the nineteenth century caught her eye, she pursued it first by examining two general histories of women's education and then by looking at specific articles on the topic that were published at the turn of the century. Only after reading a number of these articles was Cyndi certain that there was enough material here to support an entire paper on the attitudes toward women's education in the 1890s.

The point is this: a good topic for a research paper doesn't fall ready-made into one's lap; instead, it evolves slowly, as the researcher becomes more and more familiar with the subject area. The process of finding such a topic demands patience and persistence.

3.   Be prepared to make changes in your subject

The very process of writing usually alters a writer's conception of his or her topic. Sometimes the topic becomes narrower, as the writer becomes aware of the need to balance completeness with limitations on length. Sometimes it changes focus, as the writer thinks of related subjects and ideas. In research, many of these modifications of your topic will occur before you begin writing, during the research process itself.

As you start to explore a tentative subject, you must be ready to accept changes in your original plan. You should expect your research to lead in directions you had not anticipated, to new sources of information and new ideas that will inevitably affect your original conception of your topic. The opinions of others will modify your early ideas, leaving you with new perspectives to consider. On other occasions, unfortunately, you may find that the libraries available to you do not have enough material on your subject from which to construct a serious research paper, and you will be forced to modify your original subject radically or to abandon it altogether. Such is the life of the dedicated researcher—a combination of excitement and frustration, of discovery and disillusionment.

1c   Thinking about your reader

Professional researchers write with a keen awareness of their potential readers. Typically, scholars begin a research project with a specific journal in mind to which they plan eventually to submit the finished project for publication. They know what sorts of people read that journal and what those people probably already know about the subject. They also know whether they are elaborating on someone else's research or contradicting it, and as a result they have a fair sense of the extent to which their work will be regarded as innovative, controversial, or revolutionary.

It's very possible that your own professional work after college will place you in a similar situation. Whether you do research for publication in a professional journal or for in-house distribution to colleagues in a business setting, you will be writing for a community of readers whose potential reactions to your research will be constantly in your mind. For this assignment, however, your sole audience is likely to be your instructor. How can awareness of this audience affect what you write?

Two questions about audience that writers should always keep in mind may help you in this situation as well: What does your reader already know about this subject? What else do you want your reader to know? If, in the case of your instructor, you're unsure about how to answer these questions, you should plan to discuss your paper with him or her as it evolves. Find out what your instructor knows about your subject, and what aspects of your research he or she finds particularly intriguing. Use such discussions to direct your research efforts and to shape your paper, so that in its final form it responds to your instructor's interests and questions.

1d   Planning the long paper

Perhaps the most disconcerting requirement of a research paper is its length—often five or more times longer than most of the other papers you have written in freshman composition. Writing a long paper that draws on material from different sources is good practice in the kinds of writing tasks that people in many professions are called on to complete—business reports, legal briefs, case histories, and feature articles, to name just a few. But such writing makes demands that shorter, less formal essays do not.

1.   Leave enough time

The finest library facilities and the best ideas for a research paper will not be of much use to you if you do not leave enough time to work on your paper. You may have been able to write a first draft of your other essays in freshman composition in just a few sittings— one devoted to exploring the subject, one to outlining and planning, one to composing. That approach, however, will not be sufficient for a serious research paper, which usually involves at least a few weeks of preliminary work even before you begin writing, and several composing sessions as you assimilate and structure the material you have accumulated.

You can never begin researching too early, for you must be prepared for all the setbacks that accompany research, ranging from the topic that grows increasingly complex (or that fails to develop at all) to the crucial book that you discover is missing from your library. And the task of fusing your final set of notes into a coherent whole may also be more difficult than you expect. The most important rule for research, then, is to plan ahead, leaving yourself plenty of time to gather information and several sessions for writing and revising. The research paper completed in a single coffee-soaked night is not likely to be very successful, no matter how thorough the research on which it is based.

2. Understand the research process

The research process involves a number of steps, including identifying a subject, collecting information, selecting the material you want to use, assimilating it into a coherent, focused piece of writing, and accurately documenting your sources. To work efficiently in each of these stages, you need to understand their relation to one another and to the research process as a whole. Before you begin to work on your paper, therefore, you should at least skim through the six chapters that follow.

Locating information and taking notes

The first step in composing a research paper, of course, is gathering information. For your purposes, that will mean doing substantial research in a library. You can't understand or focus your topic until you have a firm grasp of what others have written about the subject. Chapters **2** and **3** will discuss some important sources of information in the library and some strategies for taking effective notes from the material you find.

Assimilating materials and avoiding plagiarism

By definition, research draws on the work of others. One of the keys to composing a successful research paper is being able to integrate the fruits of research into your paper, smoothly incorporating the information you have collected into your own prose. A second key to successful writing based on research is distinguishing between the legitimate and illegitimate use of other people's ideas and words in your paper. Presenting such material as your own, whether deliberately or accidentally, is a serious offense known as plagiarism. Chapter **4** will deal with the artful—and accurate—use of these materials in your paper.

Using standard methods of documentation

Your instructor will no doubt specify which style of documentation he or she would prefer that you use to indicate your sources of information. This book presents three of the most widely used documentation methods. The first, discussed in Chapter **3**, is the method advocated by the Modern Language Association and used in literary study and many other humanities fields. The second, described in Chapter **6**, is prescribed by the American Psychological Association and widely used in the social sciences. The third method, involving endnote citations, is less widely used today than formerly but is still the norm in some disciplines; it is presented in Chapter **7**. Each of the sample student research papers in Chapters **5**, **6**, and **7** illustrates one of these methods.

3. Be prepared for the recursiveness of the research process

Writing is a recursive rather than a linear process, that is, a process whose stages are often cyclical rather than sequential. The same is true for the research process. You can avoid some of the frustration of doing research by preparing for the fact that composing a research paper inevitably involves backtracking: abandoning an unworkable subject and beginning anew; discarding notes that prove worthless and searching for better ones; rethinking your paper's focus again and again; returning to the library, even after you have begun writing the paper, to verify a quotation or to look for just one more source. When you feel caught in a dizzying whirl of contradictory note cards, half-completed paragraphs, citations to still unexamined sources, and maddeningly arbitrary documentation rules, you'll know that you have become a true researcher at last.

2 *The Library*

When most people think of libraries, they think of books—and with good reason, for books are the most visible of any library's holdings. When you use a library for serious research, however, you need to be familiar with the many other kinds of materials available—especially with standard reference works, magazines, journals, newspapers, and government publications. Since most American libraries use the same basic system for filing and organizing materials, you will find that the guidelines below will apply to almost any library that you have access to. But you should remember that this book offers only an introduction to library use. To get the most out of your library, you will have to discover its own particular strengths—its large microfilm holdings, for example, or its outstanding record collection. You will need to know where various holdings are kept and what library policies govern their use. You can learn about these and other features of your library through the official tours that many college libraries offer at the beginning of the semester. Or you can give yourself a tour. Ask at the main desk for a map of the building and its features, or simply wander from floor to floor at a leisurely pace, identifying the materials available and noting their locations. Becoming familiar with the arrangement and system of your library is your first task as a serious researcher, one that will help to make your work more efficient and satisfying.

2a The card catalog

The card catalog in a library is the major index to its holdings. Usually, all the books, reference works, indexes, and periodicals received by a library are indexed alphabetically here on three-by-five-inch cards.

Each book is ordinarily listed in at least three different places: under its author's name (under each author's name if there are more than one); under its title; and under the subject or subjects it covers. In some university libraries, author and title cards are collected in a single alphabetical catalog, while subject cards are filed separately, also in alphabetical order.

1. Reading catalog cards

Catalog cards contain a good deal of potentially important information, including the publication date of a book, the number of

Catalog cards

its pages, and notes about such features as indexes and illustrations in the book. The more you use the card catalog, the more skilled you will become in assessing this information before you actually examine the book itself. When you identify a book that you wish to look at, make a note of its *call number*, also found on the catalog card. The call number, which is based on a nationally used classification system, is your guide to the location of the book in your library. Two principal systems of classification are used by American libraries: the Dewey Decimal System (a numerical system) and the Library of Congress System (an alphabetical classification). At your library's main desk, you can get further information about the system your library follows. If your library has open stacks—that is, if library patrons are allowed to browse through the shelves and select books themselves—you will also find information there about the location of books throughout the library.

2. Locating books

When you want to know where a specific book is located in your library, the author or title card will lead you to it fastest. When you don't know authors or titles, look through the cards under the subject you are interested in. Since both the Dewey Decimal System and the Library of Congress System are based on subject matter, you will usually find that the books your library has on a particular subject are shelved together. You can use the subject cards, therefore, not only as a listing of the library's holdings on a subject but also as a guide to the appropriate section of the book stacks. If your library has open stacks, some browsing around in this area will usually lead you to a number of useful books. Feel free to pull down from the shelves any books that look interesting, but respect your library's policies about reshelving books. To avoid the chaos created by accidental mis-shelving, many libraries ask that you do not put books back yourself, but instead leave them on a table or at some other designated place for library staff members to reshelve.

3. Using an on-line catalog

Increasingly, libraries are developing computer systems that enable patrons to bypass the card catalog and locate books and other materials simply by typing the author or title into a computer terminal, which then displays all of the information normally found on a card in the card catalog. Some such systems also make it possible to search for books by subject. If your library has put its holdings "on line" with such a system, you should definitely learn how to use it, for it will save you valuable time. However, because subject searches on these systems can sometimes be hard to use effectively and because a library may not have all of its holdings on line, you will probably also want to be sure that you know how to locate books through the card catalog if you have to.

2b   Standard reference works

You can use the card catalog to locate not only individual books by a specific author or on a particular subject, but also the standard reference works owned by your library—encyclopedias, dictionaries, indexes, and bibliographies. Your personal library no doubt includes a number of reference books, such as a dictionary and a desk encyclopedia; a college or public library, however, may own hundreds of specialized and useful reference works. These works fall into two general categories: books that offer facts (usually in the form of compact essays on various subjects), and books that provide bibliographies (lists of other books and articles on a given subject). As we saw in Chapter **1**, reference books in the first category are a good starting place for your research efforts, for the overview of a subject that they provide will often include references to a host of interesting subtopics ideal for further exploration. Reference books in the second category will lead you to further sources of information as your research efforts begin in earnest.

Reference works, like other books, are shelved according to call number, but most libraries conveniently place their reference books together in a single section of the library, or even in a separate reference room. (The catalog card will indicate whether that is your library's practice.) As you become familiar with the reference works in your library, you may want to keep your own list or card file of the ones that you have found especially useful, so that you can locate them quickly for future research work. Skill in using your library's reference collection, like skill in most other areas of life, will come from frequent practice.

What follows is a list of some standard reference works, grouped by type and subject. You will no doubt find many more in your library.

Guides to reference books

Guide to Reference Books.
Guide to the Use of Books and Libraries.
The Reader's Adviser.

General information

Collier's Encyclopedia.
Dictionary of the History of Ideas.
Encyclopedia Americana.
Encyclopaedia Britannica.
New Columbia Encyclopedia.

Gazetteers and atlases

Columbia-Lippincott Gazetteer of the World.
National Geographic Atlas of the World.
Rand McNally Atlas of World History.
The Times Atlas of the World.

Reference books for special subjects

Art and architecture

Bryan's Dictionary of Painters and Engravers.
Encyclopedia of World Art.
Haggar, Reginald C. *Dictionary of Art Terms.*
Hamlin, T. F. *Architecture through the Ages.*
Myers, Bernard S., ed. *Encyclopedia of Painting.*
Zboinski, A., and L. Tyszynski. *Dictionary of Architecture and Building Trades.*

Biography

American Men and Women of Science. Includes scholars in the physical, biological, and social sciences.

Current Biography. Monthly since 1940, with brief bibliographic entries and an annual cumulative index.

Dictionary of American Biography. 20 vols. and supplements;
bibliographic entries at the end of each article.

Dictionary of National Biography (British). 22 vols. and supplements; each article accompanied by a bibliography.

Directory of American Scholars.

James, Edward T., and Janet W. James, eds. *Notable American
Women, 1607–1950.* Has bibliographic entries.

National Cyclopedia of American Biography. Includes supplements.

Webster's Biographical Dictionary.

Who's Who (British), *Who's Who in America, International
Who's Who.* Brief accounts of living men and women;
frequently revised.

Who's Who of American Women. 1958–.

Classics

Avery, C. B., ed. *New Century Classical Handbook.*

Hammond, N. G. L., and H. H. Scullard, eds. *Oxford Classical
Dictionary.*

Harvey, Paul, ed. *Oxford Companion to Classical Literature.*

Current events

Americana Annual. 1923–. Annual supplement to the *Encyclopedia Americana.*

Britannica Book of the Year. 1938–. Annual supplement to
the *Encyclopaedia Britannica;* some entries have a brief bibliography.

Facts on File. 1941–.

Statesman's Year Book. 1864–. A statistical and historical annual
giving current information (and brief bibliographies) about
countries of the world.

World Almanac. 1968–.

Economics and commerce

Coman, E. T. *Sources of Business Information*. A bibliography.

Greenwald, Douglas, et al. *McGraw-Hill Dictionary of Modern Economics*. Has bibliographic references.

Historical Statistics of the United States: Colonial Times to 1970. Includes indexes and bibliographies.

International Bibliography of Economics. 1952–.

Munn, Glenn G. *Encyclopedia of Banking and Finance*. Has bibliographic entries.

Sloan, Harold S., and Arnold Zurcher. *A Dictionary of Economics*.

Statistical Abstract of the United States. 1897–.

Wyckham, Robert G. *Images and Marketing: A Selected and Annotated Bibliography*.

Education

Burke, Arvid J., and Mary A. Burke. *Documentation in Education*.

Deighton, Lee C., ed. *Encyclopedia of Education*. Has bibliographic entries.

Husen, Torsten, and T. Neville Postlethwaite, eds. *International Encyclopedia of Education*.

Knowles, Asa S. *International Encyclopedia of Higher Education*.

Mitzel, Harold E., ed. *Encyclopedia of Educational Research*.

World Survey of Education.

Film

Bawden, Liz-Anne, ed. *Oxford Companion to Film*.

International Encyclopedia of Film.

History

Adams, James T., ed. *Dictionary of American History*. A bibliography accompanies each article.

American Historical Association: Guide to Historical Literature.

Cambridge Ancient History. Bibliographic footnotes.

Cambridge Medieval History. Bibliographic footnotes.

Langer, William L., ed. *Encyclopedia of World History*.

Martin, Michael R., et al. *An Encyclopedia of Latin-American History*.

Morris, Richard B., and Graham W. Irwin, eds. *Harper Encyclopedia of the Modern World*.

New Cambridge Modern History. Bibliographic footnotes.

Literature

American

Hart, J. D. *Oxford Companion to American Literature*.

Leary, Lewis. *Articles on American Literature*.

Spiller, Robert E., et al. *Literary History of the United States*. Entries include bibliographic essays.

British

Baugh, A. C., et al. *A Literary History of England*. Has bibliographic entries.

Drabble, Margaret, ed. *Oxford Companion to English Literature*.

Sampson, George. *Concise Cambridge History of English Literature*.

Watson, George, ed. *New Cambridge Bibliography of English Literature*.

Wilson, F. P., and Bonamy Dobree, eds. *Oxford History of English Literature*. Excellent bibliographic essays at the end of each volume.

General

Fleischmann, Wolfgang Bernard, ed. *Encyclopedia of World Literature in the Twentieth Century*. Brief bibliographies.

Grigson, Geoffrey. *The Concise Encyclopedia of Modern World Literature*. Brief bibliographic entries.

Leach, Maria, and Jerome Fried, eds. *Funk & Wagnall's Standard Dictionary of Folklore, Mythology, and Legend.*

MacCulloch, John A., et al. *Mythology of All Races.* Bibliography at end of each volume.

Preminger, Alex, F. J. Warnke, and O. B. Hardison, eds. *Princeton Encyclopedia of Poetry and Poetics.* A brief bibliography accompanies each article.

Toye, William, ed. *Oxford Companion to Canadian Literature.*

Music and dance

Apel, Willi. *Harvard Dictionary of Music.* Has brief bibliographic entries.

Beaumont, Cyril W. *A Bibliography of Dancing.*

De Mille, Agnes. *The Book of the Dance.*

Ewen, David. *The World of Twentieth Century Music.* Brief bibliographic entries.

Grove, George. *Dictionary of Music and Musicians.* This work and the *Harvard Dictionary of Music* are the authorities in the field. Excellent bibliographies.

Hanna, Judith Lynne. *To Dance Is Human.*

Orrey, Leslie, ed. *Encyclopedia of Opera.*

Scholes, P. A. *Oxford Companion to Music.* Includes bibliographies.

Thompson, Oscar. *International Cyclopedia of Music and Musicians.* Brief bibliographies.

Westrup, J. A., ed. *New Oxford History of Music.* Includes bibliographies.

Philosophy

Copleston, Frederick. *A History of Western Philosophy.* Bibliography at end of each volume.

Edwards, Paul, ed. *Encyclopedia of Philosophy.* Bibliographies.

Urmson, J. O. *Concise Encyclopedia of Western Philosophy and Philosophers.* Brief bibliography at end of volume.

Political science

Levy, Leonard W., ed. *Encyclopedia of the American Constitution*.

Morgenthau, Hans. *Politics among Nations*.

Political Handbook of the World. 1927–.

Smith, Edward C., and A. J. Zurcher, eds. *Dictionary of American Politics*.

White, Carl M., et al. *Sources of Information in the Social Sciences*.

Psychology

Beigel, Hugo. *Dictionary of Psychology and Related Fields*.

Corsini, Raymond J., ed. *Encyclopedia of Psychology*.

Drever, James. *Dictionary of Psychology*.

Gregory, Richard L., ed. *Oxford Companion to the Mind*.

The Harvard List of Books in Psychology. Annotated.

Psychological Abstracts. 1927–.

Wolman, Benjamin B., ed. *International Encyclopedia of Psychiatry, Psychology, Psychoanalysis, and Neurology*.

Religion

Buttrick, G. A., et al. *Interpreter's Dictionary of the Bible: An Illustrated Encyclopedia*. Has bibliographic entries.

Cross, F. L., and Elizabeth A. Livingstone. *Oxford Dictionary of the Christian Church*. Has brief bibliographies.

Eliade, Mircea, ed. *Encyclopedia of Religion*. Brief bibliographic entries.

Encyclopedia of Islam.

Encyclopedia Judaica.

Hastings, James, ed. *Encyclopedia of Religion and Ethics*.

Jackson, S. M., et al. *New Schaff-Herzog Encyclopedia of Religious Knowledge*.

Malalasekera, G. P., ed. *Encyclopedia of Buddhism*.

New Catholic Encyclopedia.

Science

General

McGraw-Hill Encyclopedia of Science and Technology.

Meyers, Robert A., ed. *Encyclopedia of Physical Science and Technology.*

Newman, James R., et al. *Harper Encyclopedia of Science.* Brief bibliographic entries.

Van Nostrand's Scientific Encyclopedia.

Life sciences

Benthall, Jonathan. *Ecology in Theory and Practice.* Includes bibliographic references.

De Bell, Garrett, ed. *The Environmental Handbook.* Bibliography at end of volume.

Gray, Peter, ed. *Encyclopedia of the Biological Sciences.* Brief bibliographic entries.

Reich, Warren T., ed. *Encyclopedia of Bioethics.*

Smith, Roger C., and W. Malcolm Reid, eds. *Guide to the Literature of the Life Sciences.*

Physical sciences

International Dictionary of Physics and Electronics.

Kemp, D. A. *Astronomy and Astrophysics: A Bibliographical Guide.*

Larousse Encyclopedia of the Earth: Geology, Paleontology, and Prehistory.

Universal Encyclopedia of Mathematics.

Van Nostrand's International Encyclopedia of Chemical Science.

Sociology and anthropology

Biennial Review of Anthropology.

International Bibliography of Sociology. 1951–.

Sills, David L., ed. *International Encyclopedia of the Social Sciences.*
Each article followed by a bibliography.
Social Work Year Book. 1929–. Includes bibliographies.

Theater

Bordman, Gerald M. *Oxford Companion to American Theatre.*
Encyclopedia of World Theater.
Gassner, John, and Edward Quin, eds. *Reader's Encyclopedia of World Drama.*
Hartnoll, Phyllis, ed. *Oxford Companion to the Theatre.* Bibliography accompanies each article.

2c Indexes to periodicals

Many students new to research rely heavily—or even exclusively—on books as their sources of information. Such a strategy has its pitfalls. For one thing, books are not usually as well focused as a narrowly defined research topic, and finding the precise information you need in a towering stack of general books on a subject can become an exercise in frustration. Moreover, the time involved in producing a book means that current information—the most recent developments in Middle Eastern politics, for example, or the latest advances in AIDS research—may not be available in book form. To find such information, in addition to material on virtually any other kind of topic, you can turn to articles in periodicals.

Just as the card catalog provides an author, title, and subject index to your library's book holdings, periodical indexes offer a fast and easy way of locating articles in magazines, journals, and newspapers. Usually, you will find your library's periodical indexes grouped together in the reference collection. It is important to know the scope of at least the major indexes described below, because they cover different kinds of periodicals. However, since many of these indexes are produced by the same publisher in similar formats, you will discover that after you have become familiar with the layout of one, you can move easily to the others. For example, note the similarities in form of the indexes illustrated on page 25. The distinguishing feature of each of these

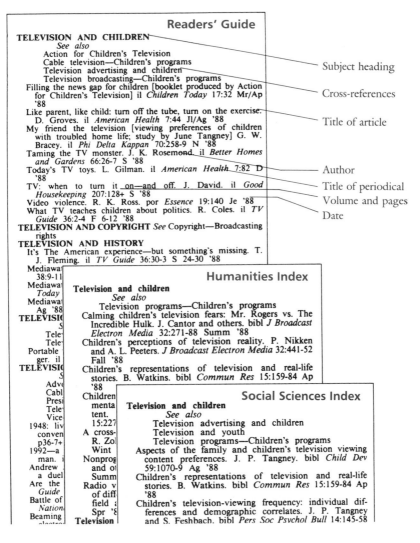

Readers' Guide

TELEVISION AND CHILDREN
  See also
  Action for Children's Television
  Cable television—Children's programs
  Television advertising and children
  Television broadcasting—Children's programs
Filling the news gap for children [booklet produced by Action for Children's Television] il *Children Today* 17:32 Mr/Ap '88
Like parent, like child: turn off the tube, turn on the exercise. D. Groves. il *American Health* 7:44 Jl/Ag '88
My friend the television [viewing preferences of children with troubled home life; study by June Tangney] G. W. Bracey. il *Phi Delta Kappan* 70:258-9 N '88
Taming the TV monster. J. K. Rosemond. il *Better Homes and Gardens* 66:26-7 S '88
Today's TV toys. L. Gilman. il *American Health* 7:82 D '88
TV: when to turn it on—and off. J. David. il *Good Housekeeping* 207:128+ S '88
Video violence. R. K. Ross. por *Essence* 19:140 Je '88
What TV teaches children about politics. R. Coles. il *TV Guide* 36:2-4 F 6-12 '88
TELEVISION AND COPYRIGHT *See* Copyright—Broadcasting rights
TELEVISION AND HISTORY
It's The American experience—but something's missing. T. J. Fleming. il *TV Guide* 36:30-3 S 24-30 '88

Mediawa[
38:9-11
Mediawa[
Today
Mediawa[
Ag '88
TELEVISI[
Tele[
Tele[
Portable [
ger. il
TELEVISI[
Adv[
Cabl
Presi
Tele[
Vice[
1948: liv
conven
p36-7+
1992—a
man. i
Andrew
a duel
Are the
Guide
Battle of
Nation[
Beaming

Subject heading
Cross-references
Title of article
Author
Title of periodical
Volume and pages
Date

Humanities Index

Television and children
  See also
  Television programs—Children's programs
Calming children's television fears: Mr. Rogers vs. The Incredible Hulk. J. Cantor and others. bibl *J Broadcast Electron Media* 32:271-88 Summ '88
Children's perceptions of television reality. P. Nikken and A. L. Peeters. *J Broadcast Electron Media* 32:441-52 Fall '88
Children's representations of television and real-life stories. B. Watkins. bibl *Commun Res* 15:159-84 Ap '88

Children
menta
tent.
15:227
A cross-
R. Zo[
Wint
Nonprog
and o[
Summ
Radio v
of diff
field
Spr '8
Television

Social Sciences Index

Television and children
  See also
  Television advertising and children
  Television and youth
  Television programs—Children's programs
Aspects of the family and children's television viewing content preferences. J. P. Tangney. bibl *Child Dev* 59:1070-9 Ag '88
Children's representations of television and real-life stories. B. Watkins. bibl *Commun Res* 15:159-84 Ap '88
Children's television-viewing frequency: individual differences and demographic correlates. J. P. Tangney and S. Feshbach. bibl *Pers Soc Psychol Bull* 14:145-58

Periodical Indexes

indexes is not the way it arranges its contents, but the distinctive type of periodical it covers.

Once you have used the indexes below to locate potentially useful articles on the subject you are researching, determine whether or not your library subscribes to the journals you need by looking them up in the card catalog. Most libraries bind back issues of periodicals like books and shelve them together in a periodical room or by call number among books in the stacks. Current issues are usually on display in a periodicals reading room. For assistance in locating the periodicals you need, ask at your library's main desk.

If your library does not have a specific periodical that you need, ask at the Interlibrary Loan department about acquiring a photocopy of the article you're interested in from another library. Most libraries offer this service for a small charge. However, you should try not to depend on articles that you must order in this way. Unless your library can obtain copies of articles by fax, the ordering process can take several weeks, and the article, when it arrives, may turn out to be of less value to you than its title promised.

General periodical indexes

Readers' Guide to Periodical Literature. 1900–.
An author and subject index to more than two hundred magazines of general interest, such as *Consumer Reports, Ms., Newsweek, Sports Illustrated,* and *Popular Electronics.* Bound volumes cover a year or more; paperback supplements keep the index current usually to within a few weeks.

Humanities Index and *Social Sciences Index.* 1974–. Formerly a single index, published as the *Social Sciences and Humanities Index* from 1965 to 1974, and as the *International Index* from 1907 to 1965. The major general index to professional journals in the humanities (for example, *American Literature, Harvard Theological Review, Journal of Philosophy, New England Quarterly*) and the social sciences (for example, *Crime and Delinquency, Geographical Review, Journal of Economic Theory, Political Science Quarterly*). Same format as the *Readers' Guide,* though usually somewhat less current.

New York Times Index. 1913–.

An invaluable subject and author index to one of the world's great newspapers. Provides a brief summary of most articles, together with a citation to issue date, section, and page. Most libraries carry the *New York Times* on microfilm; for the location of microfilms in your library and instructions on their use, ask at the main desk or in the reference room. If you live in an area served by another major newspaper, your library may also have an index for it that will help you find information on significant current and past events in your community.

Nineteenth Century Readers' Guide. 1890–99.

A two-volume supplement to the *Readers' Guide,* produced in the same format.

Poole's Index to Periodical Literature. 1802–1906.

A six-volume index of nineteenth-century periodicals by subject only. For authors, consult the *Cumulative Author Index for Poole's Index to Periodical Literature,* ed. C. Edward Wall (Ann Arbor: Pierian Press, 1971).

Biography Index. 1946–.

A subject index to articles and sections of books that are biographical in character. Note that an effective search requires consulting every volume. Same format as the *Readers' Guide.*

Subject periodical indexes

Many disciplines produce thorough indexes to a variety of specialized journals in the field. Whenever your research is within a specific academic discipline, you should check to see whether such an index exists. The indexes that follow, and others like them, can be located through the library's card catalog; you will usually find them shelved near the general periodical indexes described above. Most use the same format as the *Readers' Guide.*

Applied Science and Technology Index. 1957–.

Art Index. 1929–.

Biological Abstracts. 1926–.

Business Periodicals Index. 1958–.

Current Anthropology. 1960–.
Economic Abstracts. 1953–.
Education Index. 1929–.
Engineering Index. 1884–.
General Science Index. 1978–.
Historical Abstracts. 1955–.
Music Index. 1949–.
Philosopher's Index. 1940–.
Modern Language Association International Bibliography. 1956–.
   Formerly the *MLA American Bibliography,* 1921–55.
   The major bibliography of articles on English, American,
   and foreign language and literature.
Psychological Abstracts. 1927–.
Public Affairs Information Service. 1915–.
   A valuable index of articles, books, pamphlets, government
   documents, and other reports on public administration,
   international relations, and a broad range of economic
   and social issues.
Religious Index One: Periodicals. 1973–.
Sociological Abstracts. 1955–.
Zoological Record. 1864–.

2d   A special index: the *Essay and General Literature Index*

   This is an appropriate place to mention one other unusual
index—not an index to periodicals, but an index to *sections* of books.
The *Essay and General Literature Index* (1900–), whose location you
can find in the card catalog, is a semiannual subject and author index
to collections of essays on different subjects, often written by different
authors. This index is usually the only way to locate such essays, since
the title and subject classification of these books in the card catalog
will ordinarily not be specific enough to help you.
   Suppose, for example, that you are interested in the subject of
women and art. If you look under the two headings "Women" and

"Art" in the card catalog, you will find dozens of books on each subject, but you might spend days—or even weeks—looking through the books on women for those that also deal with art, and searching in the books on art for material on women artists. A few minutes of browsing in a recent issue of the *Essay and General Literature Index,* however, will lead you to the heading "Women in Art," and under it, entries like the following:

> Withers, J. Judy Chicago's Dinner party: a personal vision of women's history. *In* Art the ape of nature, ed. by M. Barasch and L. F. Sandler p789–99

What this entry means is that an essay by J. Withers entitled "Judy Chicago's Dinner Party: A Personal Vision of Women's History" is included on pages 789–99 of the book *Art, the Ape of Nature,* edited by M. Barasch and L. F. Sandler. The complete publication information for any book that you find listed is included at the back of the volume of the *Essay and General Literature Index* that you are using. With this information, you can go to the card catalog and determine whether the book is available in your library. Typically, a library would list this book in the card catalog only under its title, the names of its two editors, and the broad subject heading "Art—Addresses, Essays, and Lectures." Without the *Essay and General Literature Index,* you would have no easy way of finding Withers's essay.

2e Data-base searches

An increasing number of libraries offer their patrons computerized access to lists of articles, unpublished papers, and other sources of information on a wide variety of subjects. Such computerized files are known as **data bases.** Many college and university libraries provide access to such data bases in one or both of the following ways.

1. On-line searches

Libraries may subscribe to the services of a data-base "vendor," a company that makes available by computer the contents of many different data bases compiled and updated by independent companies and associations. For example, DIALOG, one of the largest such vendors, currently offers access to nearly two hundred separate data bases in business, technology, the humanities, the social sciences, and the natural sciences. In all, a DIALOG subscriber may search through more than seventy-five million records for titles relevant to a specific subject.

Conducting an on-line search

To perform a data-base search in most libraries, you will be asked by the reference librarian to complete an information form on your subject. The librarian will then enter one or more "descriptors," or relevant subject headings, into a computer terminal, and the computer will search through all of the data bases on the system and compile a list of appropriate sources. On some systems, moreover, you can order a printed copy of the full text of an article. Some libraries also subscribe to simplified searching systems that library patrons can use directly, without the intermediary help of a librarian.

The only drawback to such on-line searching is the cost, which is usually calculated according to the length of time you are connected to the computer system. Although a ten-minute computer search may cost only a few dollars, a search that takes considerably longer can become an unrealistically expensive proposition for undergraduate research. On the other hand, data-base searches offer enormous savings of time. In just a few minutes, a computer can scan bibliographies that might take weeks to examine by hand. On-line data bases are also more current than printed reference works can be. The Wilsonline data bases, for example, which offer computerized access to the Wilson family of periodical indexes (*Readers' Guide, Humanities Index, Social Science Index, Biography Index, Education Index,* etc.), are updated twice each week, whereas the corresponding bound indexes usually lag several weeks to several months behind the current date.

Additional on-line data bases

Below is a list of some other widely used on-line data bases. Check with your reference librarian to determine whether these or similar on-line data bases are available at your library.

Arts and Humanities Search
Indexes more than thirteen hundred journals in the humanities, beginning in 1980.

Dissertation Abstracts Online
Indexes American dissertations in all disciplines, beginning in 1861.

PsycINFO
Indexes more than a thousand journals in psychology, beginning in 1967.

Scisearch
Indexes a variety of journals in science and technology, beginning in 1974.

Social Scisearch
Indexes more than fifteen hundred social science journals, beginning in 1972.

2. CD-ROM searches

Many data bases are also available on laser-read compact discs, similar to the compact discs used for recording and playing back music. Libraries that receive data bases on such discs (referred to as *CD-ROM*, for "compact disc, read-only memory") often make them directly available to patrons at no charge.

For example, most of the Wilson periodicals, including the *Readers' Guide*, the *Humanities Index*, and the *Social Sciences Index*, are available for CD-ROM searches. All the records contained in each of these indexes since 1983 (or in some cases 1984) have been recorded on a single compact disc that is replaced with an updated version four times a year. The disc's contents are read by laser and displayed on an ordinary computer terminal. But a CD-ROM search is more than a computerized version of the browsing you might do in the printed volumes of one of these indexes. Using a command called Wilsearch, you can perform a very powerful kind of subject search that is possible only on a computer.

Using Wilsearch

The Wilsearch request menu asks you to enter up to eight descriptive words covering the topic you are interested in. The more terms you enter, the more precise—but also the more limited—your search will be. The computer then searches all of the records on the compact disc (that is, all of the articles indexed since 1983 or 1984), looking for any articles that have in common all the terms you've

Wilsearch
request
menu

```
Enter your search request for HUM

Subject words: education
  2nd subject: women
  3rd subject:

  Author/name:
  Title words:

  Journal name:
  Organization:
  Dewey number:

  Press Enter key to perform search

  ┌──────────────────────────────────────────────────┐
  │ You do not need to fill out the entire screen. Use │
  │ only those lines appropriate to your search request.│
  └──────────────────────────────────────────────────┘
```

Search identifies
eighty articles
on women and
education

```
                    WILSONDISC - WILSEARCH
    FILE:HUM - Humanities Index 2/84-06/30/89              READY
    ----------------------------------------------------------
    SEARCH                                              NUMBER of
    SET   |  STEP  |  FORMULATION                    |  POSTINGS
    ----------------------------------------------------------
      1   |    1   |  FIND EDUCATION(BI)             |    1055
      2   |    2   |  FIND WOMEN(BI)                 |    3506
      3   |    3   |  FIND 1 AND 2                   |      80
          |        |          (ss #1)... 1055 Postings |
          |        |          (ss #2)... 3506 Postings |

      ┌──────────────────────────────┐
      │  80 CITATIONS FOUND          │
      │ HIT ⏎ ENTER                  │
      └──────────────────────────────┘
```

Publication
information
for one entry

```
  1 HUM
Book Review
  Arnold, Lois
Four lives in science; women's education in the
nineteenth century
reviewed by McGrath, Sylvia Wallace
The Journal of American History 72: 416 S '85
```

Searching a CD-ROM Data Base with Wilsearch

indicated. If it finds any matches, it displays the full citations one at a time and gives you the opportunity to print out a copy of any entries that interest you.

Suppose, for example, that you, like Cyndi, are interested in women's education in the nineteenth century. Using the Wilsondisc for the *Humanities Index,* you might begin by entering just two of your key terms, *education* and *women.* (See the illustrations on page 32.) The computer then reads the disc and in this case identifies a total of eighty articles indexed since February 1984 that involve both of these subjects. To narrow the search, you could enter a third key word, *nineteenth century.* The computer would then identify and display the titles of articles that include all three key terms, like the one shown in the illustration.

Additional CD-ROM data bases

Similar searching capabilities are available on a variety of other CD-ROM data bases, such as those listed below. To determine whether your library subscribes to these or other CD-ROM data bases, check with your reference librarian.

Academic Index
Indexes nearly four hundred journals and magazines considered likely to be used in undergraduate research. Includes citations to periodicals in the humanities, the social sciences, business, education, psychology, and biology, as well as citations to general interest magazines. Some citations begin as early as 1985. Also includes citations to the *New York Times* for the most recent six-month period. Updated monthly.

ERIC
An index of materials available through the Educational Resources Information Center, including published journal articles and unpublished research reports.

Infotrac Magazine Index Plus
Indexes more than four hundred widely read magazines such as those indexed in the *Readers' Guide,* beginning in 1983. Includes citations to the *New York Times* for the most recent three-month period. Updated monthly.

Newspaper Abstracts Ondisc
An index to the *New York Times,* the *Chicago Tribune,* the *Wall Street Journal,* and the *Christian Science Monitor,* beginning in 1985.

2f   Government documents

One of the most often overlooked and yet one of the most valuable sources of information on a wide range of subjects is the

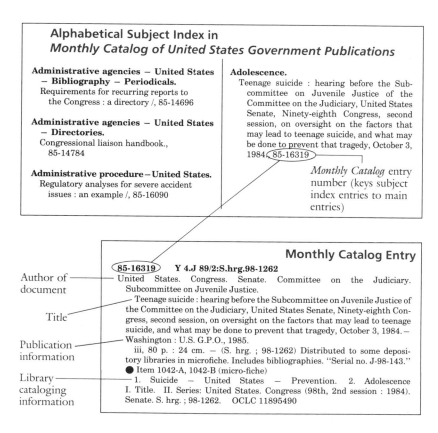

Alphabetical Subject Index in
Monthly Catalog of United States Government Publications

Administrative agencies – United States – Bibliography – Periodicals.
Requirements for recurring reports to the Congress : a directory /, 85-14696

Administrative agencies – United States – Directories.
Congressional liaison handbook., 85-14784

Administrative procedure – United States.
Regulatory analyses for severe accident issues : an example /, 85-16090

Adolescence.
Teenage suicide : hearing before the Subcommittee on Juvenile Justice of the Committee on the Judiciary, United States Senate, Ninety-eighth Congress, second session, on oversight on the factors that may lead to teenage suicide, and what may be done to prevent that tragedy, October 3, 1984. 85-16319

Monthly Catalog entry number (keys subject index entries to main entries)

Monthly Catalog Entry

85-16319   Y 4.J 89/2:S.hrg.98-1262
Author of document — United States. Congress. Senate. Committee on the Judiciary. Subcommittee on Juvenile Justice.
Title — Teenage suicide : hearing before the Subcommittee on Juvenile Justice of the Committee on the Judiciary, United States Senate, Ninety-eighth Congress, second session, on oversight on the factors that may lead to teenage suicide, and what may be done to prevent that tragedy, October 3, 1984. – Washington : U.S. G.P.O., 1985.
Publication information — iii, 80 p. : 24 cm. – (S. hrg. ; 98-1262) Distributed to some depository libraries in microfiche. Includes bibliographies. "Serial no. J-98-143."
● Item 1042-A, 1042-B (micro-fiche)
Library cataloging information — 1. Suicide – United States – Prevention. 2. Adolescence I. Title. II. Series: United States. Congress (98th, 2nd session : 1984). Senate. S. hrg. ; 98-1262.   OCLC 11895490

Locating Government Documents

U.S. government. Each year, the agencies of the national government publish thousands of pamphlets, booklets, magazines, and books on hundreds of subjects. Many libraries routinely receive and catalog much of this material, which is usually collected together in a single location.

The subject index in the *Monthly Catalog of United States Government Publications* is a good place to begin discovering the range and variety of government documents. The subject headings in one recent issue include everything from "Acid Rain" to "Airplane Inspection," from "Computer Graphics" to "Chippewa Indians," from "Lake Trout" to "Literacy," from "Radioactive Waste Disposal" to "Retirement" to "Rhetoric" to "Rocket Engines." Once you have located some promising titles in the subject index, the government documents librarian in your library can show you how to use the index to the documents on file and how to find items in your library's collection.

EXERCISE 1

Choose several of the subjects below and read the entries about them in *Collier's Encyclopedia*, the *Encyclopedia Americana*, and the *Encyclopaedia Britannica* (check both sections, the *Micropaedia* and the more detailed *Macropaedia*). Which encyclopedia's coverage seems generally most complete? Which one seems most up to date? Which supplies the best bibliographies of additional sources?

1. aging	9. Navajo/Navaho
2. crime	10. Normans
3. cocaine	11. Frances Perkins
4. Detroit	12. sextant
5. fencing	13. surfing
6. greenhouse effect	14. Louis Tiffany
7. humor	15. trademark
8. Jerusalem	

EXERCISE 2

Use the *Readers' Guide* to locate the earliest magazine article available in your library on one of the subjects below. Look up the article, read through it, and write a short essay explaining how our conception of the subject has changed since it was published.

1. AIDS
2. microwave cooking
3. Ronald Reagan
4. stereo
5. television

Working with Sources

A list of books, articles, and other sources of information on a given topic is called a bibliography. Most research papers end with a bibliography or with a list of all the works the writer has referred to in the paper. But the research process also *begins* with the compilation of a "working bibliography," that is, a list of sources that the writer intends to examine. Only after assembling such a preliminary list of sources do most researchers move to the next important stage of research, taking notes.

3a The working bibliography

The working bibliography is valuable for a number of reasons. First, it becomes your master list of sources. Over a period of several weeks of research, you will not be able to remember all of the books and articles that you consulted, some of which were useful and some of which you found irrelevant to your topic. The working bibliography offers a systematic way of keeping track of all of these sources. Because it contains references to sources that you must still check, it provides an outline of the research work that remains for you to do; and since it includes the sources you have looked at, it helps to eliminate accidental backtracking. Second, the working bibliography gives you a place to make potentially useful notes about your sources as you examine them. Later, when you are putting your paper together, you will often find it helpful to be able to recall what an author's main point in an article was, or what your reactions to a book were as you read it.

1.   Assembling a working bibliography

Use common sense in choosing items for your working bibliography. Don't waste time, for example, in collecting references to obscure publications not available in your library. Interlibrary loans are possible but may be time-consuming, unpredictable, and expensive; you will usually find it more rewarding to explore the resources of your own library. Look for information in the most likely places. If your topic is a recent event or a living person, for instance, start with newspapers and periodicals rather than with books.

The most sensible way to compile your working bibliography is to enter each potentially important source that you identify on a separate three-by-five-inch card or slip of paper. On the back of each card, make your brief notes about the source. The separate cards can be sorted in any number of handy ways; for example, you might place all the sources remaining to be consulted on the top, all those you have already examined on the bottom. When you are at last ready to prepare your paper's concluding bibliography (or *Works Cited* list, as it is frequently called), you can simply remove cards for the sources not used in the paper, alphabetize the remaining cards, and type the Works Cited list directly from them.

2.   Recording bibliographic information

In order to be able to use your working bibliography cards as the basis of your paper's final Works Cited list, you must be careful to include all the information needed for the bibliography entries when you fill out each card. Otherwise, you will find yourself trekking back to the library at the last minute to look up a missing year of publication or to double-check an illegibly written author's name. The best plan, as you fill out each bibliography card, is to use the precise bibliographic *form* described below, in order to expedite typing the Works Cited list from your original cards.

Bibliography forms vary from discipline to discipline, but most systems of citing and listing sources aim for clarity and simplicity. None is inherently superior to another. This chapter and the next two will follow the system of documentation and bibliographic (Works Cited) forms prescribed by the Modern Language Association (MLA) and used in many humanities fields. Chapters **6** and **7** will illustrate

Author's name in — *Judge, Joseph. "Florence Rises from*
inverted order   *the Flood." National Geographic*

First and   *July 1967 : 1 – 43.*
last pages
of article

Anonymous source —   *"Slow Art Restoration Continues in*
begins with title   *Florence." New York Times*

Indent second and —   *9 Aug. 1967, late city ed.: 42.*
subsequent lines

Working bibliography cards

illustrate two other systems of documentation. The most important
thing about using any such system is that you must follow it precisely
and consistently. Though its rules are arbitrary, they cannot arbitrarily
be broken.

3b MLA Works Cited forms

On the following pages you will find model MLA Works
Cited forms for most of the sources you are likely to encounter. Remember to have these samples at hand when you are compiling your working
bibliography so that you can refer to them as you fill out your bibliography cards. Note that the author's name is always given last name first
for easy indexing. For the same reason, the second and subsequent
lines of each entry are always indented. (For additional information
about MLA Works Cited forms, see Joseph Gibaldi and Walter S.
Achtert, *MLA Handbook for Writers of Research Papers*, 3rd ed. [New
York: MLA, 1988].)

Table of MLA Works Cited forms

Books
  1. Book by one author
  2. Book by two or more authors

3. Book by a committee, commission, association, or other group
4. Anonymous book
5. Later or revised edition of a book
6. Edited book (*author's work is being cited*)
7. Edited book (*editor's work is being cited*)
8. Translated book (*author's work is being cited*)
9. Translated book (*translator's work is being cited*)
10. Book in more than one volume
11. Republished book
12. Book that is part of a series
13. Book published by a division of a press
14. Book published before 1900
15. Book with incomplete publication information

Parts of books

16. Introduction, preface, foreword, or afterword in a book
17. Essay in a collection of essays by various authors
18. Poem, short story, or other work in an anthology
19. Journal or magazine article reprinted in a collection of essays by various authors

Articles in journals and magazines

20. Article in a journal paginated by the volume (*continuous pagination*)
21. Article in a journal paginated issue by issue
22. Article in a journal with issue numbers only
23. Article in a weekly or biweekly magazine
24. Article in a monthly or bimonthly magazine

Articles in newspapers

25. Article in a newspaper
26. Editorial in a newspaper
27. Letter to the editor

Other print sources

28. Abstract in *Dissertation Abstracts International*
29. Book review

30. Dissertation, unpublished
31. Encyclopedia article (*or article in similar reference work*)
32. Government document
33. Interview, published
34. Map
35. Pamphlet
36. Proceedings of a conference

Nonprint sources

37. Computer software
38. Film
39. Interview, personal
40. Lecture
41. Microfilm or microfiche
42. Recording
43. Television program
44. Videotape

Books

1. **Book by one author**

```
Novarr, David.  The Lines of Life: Theories of Biog-
        raphy, 1880-1970.  West Lafayette: Purdue UP,
        1986.
```

- A colon separates the book's main title and subtitle.
- The abbreviation *UP* means "University Press." For nonacademic publishers, use a shortened form of the company's name: *Heath* for D. C. Heath and Company, *Knopf* for Alfred A. Knopf, Inc., and so on.

2. **Book by two or more authors**

```
Scholes, Robert, and Robert Kellogg.  The Nature of
        Narrative.  London: Oxford UP, 1966.
```

- When more than one city of publication is given, use only the first in your citation (the title page of this book also lists Oxford and New York).
- In listing the authors' names, follow the same order used on the book's title page.
- Give the second author's name in normal rather than inverted order.
- If there are three authors, list both of the last two authors' names in normal order: Davis, Jane, Lee O'Brien, and Sylvia Mattheson.
- If there are more than three authors, you need give the name only of the first, following it by the Latin abbreviation *et al.* ("and others"), not underlined: Walker, Stephen A., et al.

3. Book by a committee, commission, association, or other group

American Automobile Association. Illinois/Indi-

   ana/Ohio Tour Book. Falls Church: American Au-

   tomobile Assn., 1987.

Ground Zero. Nuclear War: What's in It for You? New

   York: Pocket, 1982.

- A parenthetical text citation for either of these books would begin with the joint author's name: (American Automobile Association 44), (Ground Zero 169). See **4c**.

4. Anonymous book

Kodak Guide to 35mm Photography. Rochester: Eastman

   Kodak, 1980.

- A parenthetical text citation for this book would begin with a shortened form of the title: (Kodak Guide 16). See **4c**.

5. Later or revised edition of a book

Miller, Casey, and Kate Swift. The Handbook of Nonsexist Writing. 2nd ed. New York: Harper,
1988.

Townsend, John Rowe. Written for Children: An Outline of English-Language Children's Literature. Rev. ed. Philadelphia: Lippincott,
1975.

6. Edited book (*author's work is being cited*)

Gaskell, Elizabeth. The Life of Charlotte
Brontë. Ed. Alan Shelston. Harmondsworth:
Penguin, 1975.

Pope, Alexander. The Poems of Alexander Pope. Ed.
John Butt. New Haven: Yale UP, 1963.

- When you are citing the work of the author, put the editor's name after the title.

7. Edited book (*editor's work is being cited*)

Garber, Frederick, ed. The Italian. By Ann Radcliffe. London: Oxford UP, 1968.

Marshall, Sam A., ed. 1990 Photographer's Market.
Cincinnati: Writer's Digest Books, 1989.

- When you are citing the work of an editor, put the author's name (if one exists) after the title.

8. Translated book (*author's work is being cited*)

Brumm, Ursula. <u>American Thought and Religious</u>
<u>Typology</u>. Trans. John Hoaglund. New Bruns-
wick: Rutgers UP, 1970.

9. Translated book (*translator's work is being cited*)

Lind, L. R., trans. <u>The Aeneid</u>. By Vergil. Bloomington: Indiana UP, 1962.

10. Book in more than one volume

Sturzo, Luigi. <u>Church and State</u>. 2 vols. Notre
Dame: U of Notre Dame P, 1962.
Johnson, Edgar. <u>Sir Walter Scott: The Great</u>
<u>Unknown</u>. Vol. 1. New York: Macmillan, 1970.
2 vols.

- If you use only one volume of a book published in multiple volumes, indicate the volume you are using after the title, and end the entry with the total number of volumes in the set.

11. Republished book

Shirer, William L. <u>Berlin Diary: The Journal of a</u>
<u>Foreign Correspondent 1934–1941</u>. 1941. Har-
mondsworth: Penguin, 1979.

- The copyright page of this paperbound book indicates that it was originally issued in 1941 by a different publisher. Information about the first publisher is not required in this citation, but the original publication date is given after the title.

12. Book that is part of a series

```
Radley, Virginia L. Samuel Taylor Coleridge.
     Twayne's English Authors Ser. 36. New York:
     Twayne, 1966.
```

- Give the name of the series and, if provided, the number of the volume in the series before you list the publication information.

13. Book published by a division of a press

```
Ehrenreich, Barbara, and Deirdre English. For Her
     Own Good: 150 Years of the Experts' Advice to
     Women. Garden City: Anchor-Doubleday, 1979.
McDonnell, Thomas P., ed. A Thomas Merton Reader.
     Rev. ed. Garden City: Image-Doubleday, 1974.
```

- When a book is published by a division of a publishing house, give the name of the division first, followed by a hyphen and the name of the publisher.

14. Book published before 1900

```
Kellogg, Brainerd. A Text-Book on Rhetoric. New
     York, 1897.
```

- In citations to books published before 1900, the publisher's name may be omitted. Use a comma, not a colon, between the place of publication and the date.

15. Book with incomplete publication information

Marr, George S. The Periodical Essayists of the
Eighteenth Century. London: Clarke, n.d.

- The abbreviation *n.d.* means "no date."
- If the place of publication is missing, substitute the abbreviation *N.p.* ("no place"); if the publisher's name is missing, use the abbreviation *n.p.* ("no publisher"). The citation for a book with no publication information would be as follows: N.p. : n.p., n.d.

Parts of books

16. Introduction, preface, foreword, or afterword in a book

Miller, J. Hillis. Introduction. Bleak House. By
Charles Dickens. Ed. Norman Page. Harmondsworth: Penguin, 1971. 11–34.

17. Essay in a collection of essays by various authors

Young, Richard E. "Concepts of Art and the Teaching
of Writing." The Rhetorical Tradition and
Modern Writing. Ed. James J. Murphy. New
York: Modern Lang. Assn., 1982. 130–41.

- Follow the title of the essay with the title of the book in which it appears and the name of the book's editor or editors.
- End the entry with the first and last pages on which the essay is found.

18. Poem, short story, or other work in an anthology

Raleigh, Walter. "The Advice." The Anchor Anthol-

ogy of Sixteenth-Century Verse. Ed. Richard

S. Sylvester. New York: Anchor-Doubleday,

1974. 330-31.

- End the entry with the first and last pages on which the work in question is found.

19. Journal or magazine article reprinted in a collection of essays by various authors

Fogle, Richard Harter. "The Abstractness of Shel-

ley." Philological Quarterly 24 (1945): 362-

79. Rpt. in Shelley: A Collection of Critical

Essays. Ed. George M. Ridenour. Twentieth

Century Views. Englewood Cliffs: Prentice,

1965. 13-29.

- Provide information about an article's earlier publication when it is noted in the collection you are using. *Rpt. in* ("reprinted in") indicates that the reprinted version of this article is the one being cited.

Articles in journals and magazines

20. Article in a journal paginated by the volume (*continuous pagination*)

Miller, Jerome A. "Horror and the Deconstruction of

the Self." Philosophy Today 32 (1988): 286-98.

- Most periodicals published quarterly or less frequently use continuous pagination for all the issues published in a single year; that is, if the year's first issue ends with page 125, the second issue begins with page 126. The citation to such a periodical includes the name of the journal, the volume number (32), the year of publication (1988), and the first and last pages of the article (286–98).

21. Article in a journal paginated issue by issue

```
Butterick, George.  "Charles Olson's 'The Kingfish-
      ers' and the Poetics of Change."  American Po-
      etry 6.2 (1989): 28-59.
```

- When each issue of a journal begins with page 1, the citation includes the volume (6) *and* the issue number (2), in addition to the year of publication and the first and last pages of the article.
- A title ordinarily enclosed in double quotation marks appears in single quotation marks when it is part of a larger title enclosed in quotation marks.

22. Article in a journal with issue numbers only

```
Jacobson, Paul.  "Temperature and Your Guitar's
      Health."  Guitar Review 75 (1988): 17-18.
```

- When a periodical uses issue numbers but no volume numbers, give the issue number (75) as if it were a volume number. Compare with item 20 above.

23. Article in a weekly or biweekly magazine

```
Rudolph, Barbara.  "Adrift in the Doldrums."  Time
      31 July 1989: 32-34.
```

- Follow the title of the magazine by listing the date in inverted form, a colon, and the first and last pages of the article. Abbreviate months, except for May, June, and July.
- Begin the citation to an anonymous article with the title.

24. Article in a monthly or bimonthly magazine

```
Blakely, Mary Kay.  "Coma: Stories from the Edge of

     Death."  Life Aug. 1989: 80-88.
```

- For a bimonthly magazine, include both months, abbreviated if possible, connected by a hyphen: Jan.-Feb. 1990: 23-28.

Articles in newspapers

25. Article in a newspaper

```
Donoghue, Denis.  "Does America Have a Major Poet?"

     New York Times 3 Dec. 1978, late city ed., sec.

     7: 9+.

"GM Plans Taiwan Office."  Wall Street Journal 11

     July 1989: B2.
```

- Specify the edition of the newspaper when it is indicated on the masthead.
- If the newspaper is divided into separately paginated sections, specify the section. If the sections of the newspaper are lettered, the section can be incorporated into the page citation (B2).
- Indicate an article continued on nonconsecutive pages with a plus sign after the first page of the article (9+).
- Begin the citation to an anonymous article with the headline or title.

26. Editorial in a newspaper

"'Restraint' Spurs Terrorists." Editorial. <u>Chi-</u>
<u>cago Sun-Times</u> 3 Aug. 1989: 42.

• A signed editorial begins with the author's name in inverted order.

27. Letter to the editor

Hayden, Lavonna. "Broadway Blues." Letter. <u>Vil-</u>
<u>lage Voice</u> 28 Feb. 1989: 4.

• The title "Broadway Blues" has been supplied by the editor. Not all published letters are given titles.

Other print sources

28. Abstract in *Dissertation Abstracts International*

Krantz, Susan Ellen. "The First Fortune: The Plays
and the Playhouse." <u>DAI</u> 47 (1986): 189A. Tulane U.

29. Book review

Pettit, Norma. Rev. of <u>American Puritanism: Faith</u>
<u>and Practice</u>, by Darrett B. Rutman. <u>New En-</u>
<u>gland Quarterly</u> 43 (1970): 504-06.

• If the review has a title, put it in quotation marks after the author's name.

30. Dissertation, unpublished

Rauff, James Vernon. "Machine Translation with Two-
   Level Grammars." Diss. Northwestern U, 1988.

31. Encyclopedia article (*or article in similar reference work*)

"Phonetics." Encyclopaedia Britannica: Micropaedia. 15th ed. 1986.

Dunn, Mary Maples. "Penn, William." Encyclopedia
   of American Biography. Ed. John A. Garraty.
   New York: Harper, 1974.

- For familiar reference works such as standard encyclopedias, include the name of the author of the article (if the article is signed), the title of the entry, the name of the encyclopedia, and its edition (if given) and year of publication.
- For less familiar reference works, supply full publication information.
- Omit page and volume numbers in either type of citation when the work is organized alphabetically.

32. Government document

United States. Superintendent of Documents.
   Poetry and Literature. Washington: GPO,
   1978.

- Unless the name of the author of a government publication is given, begin the citation with the name of the government and the name of the agency issuing the document.
- *GPO* is an abbreviation of "Government Printing Office."

33. Interview, published

> Drabble, Margaret. Interview. <u>Interviews with</u>
>
>   <u>Contemporary Novelists</u>. By Diana Cooper–
>
>   Clark. New York: St. Martin's, 1986. 47–73.
>
> Stern, Gerald. "A Poet of the Mind: An Interview with
>
>   Gerald Stern." By Elizabeth Knight. <u>Poetry</u>
>
>   <u>East</u> 26 (1988): 32–48.

- Begin citations to interviews with the name of the person interviewed.
- Identify the citation as an interview if it is untitled and provide the name of the interviewer, if known, together with standard publication information.

34. Map

> <u>Southeastern States</u>. Map. Falls Church: American
>
>   Automobile Assn., 1988.

35. Pamphlet

> Rusinow, Dennison I. <u>Yugoslavia's Muslim Nation</u>.
>
>   Hanover: Universities Field Staff Intl.,
>
>   1982.

- The citation form for a pamphlet is the same as that for a book.

36. Proceedings of a conference

> Rousseas, Stephen W., ed. <u>Inflation: Its Causes,</u>
>
>   <u>Consequences and Control</u>. A Symposium Held by

the Dept. of Economics, New York U. 31 Jan.

1968. Wilton: K. Kazanjian Economics Founda-

tion, 1968.

- Include the title and date of the conference before the publication information.

Nonprint sources

37. Computer software

Etter, Thomas, and William Chamberlain. Racter.

Computer software. Mindscape, 1984.

- If the software is available in different versions, indicate the version you are citing after the name of the program: Vers. 2.2.

38. Film

Casablanca. Dir. Michael Curtiz. With Humphrey Bo-

gart, Ingrid Bergman, and Claude Rains. Warner

Bros., 1942.

39. Interview, personal

Toulouse, Teresa A. Personal interview. 31 Mar.

1985.

40. Lecture

Catano, James V. "The Paradox Behind the Myth of

Self-Making: Self-Empowerment vs. the Power of

the Academy." Conference on College Composi-

tion and Communication. Seattle, 17 Mar. 1989.

41. Microfilm or microfiche

When citing a publication reproduced on microfilm or microfiche, simply use the ordinary citation form appropriate for that publication.

42. Recording

Friendly, Fred W., and Walter Cronkite, eds. The Way

   It Was: The Sixties. Narr. Walter Cronkite.

   CBS, F3M 38858, 1983.

Barbieri, Gato, tenor sax. Tropico. Audiotape.

   A&M, CS-4710, 1978.

43. Television program

Nightline. ABC. WLS, Chicago. 23 Jan. 1990.

"Baka: People of the Forest." Writ. and prod. Phil

   Agland. National Geographic. PBS. WTTW, Chi-

   cago. 7 Aug. 1989.

- The basic information in a citation to a television program is the title of the program, the network, the local station and city, and the date. For a specific episode of a program, begin with the episode's title.
- Information about the production of a program (writer, producer, director, narrator, etc.) may be included when appropriate.

44. Videotape

The Beggar's Opera. Videocassette. By John Gay.

   Prod. and dir. Jonathan Miller. With Roger

   Daltrey and Carol Hall. BBC-TV/RM Arts, 1985.

   135 min.

3c   Taking notes

After you have identified several likely sources of information on your topic, your next impulse may be to arm yourself with packages of loose-leaf paper or piles of legal tablets to be filled up with notes. But remember that you will be writing your paper directly from your notes, not from the books you've consulted (which are hard to refer to), or from the periodicals you've read (which usually cannot leave your library). The basic consideration for note taking, then, is this: how can you take notes that will be most useful and most accessible later, as you compose the paper?

1. Note cards

For most people, the answer to this question is to take notes on separate cards or slips of paper, four by six inches or larger (regular typing paper cut in half works well). The rationale for such a system is simple. Note taking is an exploratory act, not a definitive one; as you are taking notes, you can never be certain which notes you will later use and which you will not need. If your notes are on separate cards, you will later be able to sort them out, clip them together, arrange some, and discard others. You will gain a flexibility that will enormously simplify the task of organizing and writing your paper.

For such a system of note taking to work, though, each note card must be *self-contained*. It must, in other words, contain three pieces of information:

1. *A clear, complete note*
   Be certain that the single note you put on each card is sufficiently complete to make sense to you later, when you no longer have in front of you the article or book that it came from.

2. *A reference to your source*
   To ensure that you will later be able to cite sources accurately in your paper, you must include on each note card a reference to the source from which that note was taken. Don't copy all the publication information for the source onto each note card; instead, develop a system for keying the note cards to the bibliography cards in your working bibliography. For exam-

ple, you might write just the author's last name at the top of each card (but be careful to distinguish between sources if two of them share the same last name).

3. *The page number*

You must be certain that the page number or numbers from which you took the note also appear on the note card, because you will have to cite those page numbers in your final paper.

2. Types of notes

Before we discuss the content of your notes, let's consider the types of notes that you might take. There are four basic types of notes, and a single note card may contain just one or a combination of all four.

Direct quotation

Copying direct quotations onto note cards may at first seem to be the easiest way to take notes, but often it actually creates more work for you later on. Mounds of undigested quotations lacking their original contexts are usually harder to work with as you are writing your paper than incisive and thoughtful notes in your own words (see *Paraphrase,* below). Sometimes, however, you will find a writer who states his or her point so forcefully or cleverly or succinctly that you believe you might want to quote the author's own phrasing in your paper. In such cases, when you copy an author's exact words onto your note card, be certain to enclose them in quotation marks so that later, as you compose your paper, you will be able to distinguish between your own words on your note cards and the words that belong to others.

Be certain, too, that everything within the quotation marks is exactly as it appears in the original quotation; you are not free to omit or add words randomly, or to change punctuation or spelling. If you have to add a word or phrase for clarity, you must enclose the added material in square brackets ([   ]—not parentheses). If you wish to delete part of an overly long quotation, you must show the deletion with three spaced periods (. . .) called ellipses. Quotations, in short, must be handled with precision. If you fail to set them off with quotation marks, you leave yourself open to the serious charge of plagiarism,

Text of source

essentially a struggle for survival. The amenities of gracious behavior could hardly be expected to flourish in the midst of the damp and dirt of the hastily built, overcrowded shelters, the crippling illnesses, and the spiritual disabilities of homesickness, sorrow and discouragement. But the Puritan's code of good manners was an integral part of his standard of Christian conduct, and for these devout colonists, especially those among them who had been privileged to live gently in England, it must have been disheartening to see the formality of every-day communication, the respect for individual privacy, the quick concern for a troubled neighbor, and the dignity of innate self-possession, too often falter and fail under the weight of outrageous circumstance.

Tho⌐

failed

was be

Bibliography card

White, Elizabeth Wade. *Anne Bradstreet*: "The Tenth Muse." New York : Oxford UP, 1971.

Note card

Source ——— White, p. 116

Page ———

Paraphrase ——— Crude living conditions particularly hard for Puritan colonists to endure, since

Quotation ——— "the Puritan's code of good manners was an integral part of his standard of Christian conduct...."

Researcher's ——— (another example of moral tone of life in Massachusetts Bay Colony)
note to self

Source, bibliography card, note card

discussed in the next chapter (see **4b**). If you alter them without indicating the change, your instructor may penalize you for inexact handling of sources.

Paraphrase

A paraphrase is a restatement of another writer's ideas in words that are entirely your own. Paraphrasing takes thought and care, for it must reflect the meaning of the given text but be wholly original in phrasing. You may not simply replace some of the words in another writer's sentence with your own; instead, the very structure of your sentence should be different from your source's. Good paraphrasing takes time when you are doing it, but it can save time later: if you have paraphrased well, you may be able to write your paper directly from material on your note cards (though you will still need to acknowledge the source of the ideas contained in your prose). For advice on paraphrasing properly, see **4b**.

Summary

As you get further and further along in your research, you will be better able to decide when you need to note all of the details given in a passage in one of your sources and when you can simply summarize the passage in a sentence or two. Look for opportunities to use summary effectively as a way of reducing your work without sacrificing important information.

Notes to yourself

Have you found a quotation that might make an attention-getting introduction to your paper? Are you reading a source whose ideas contradict those in other articles you've examined? Is the book in front of you the best survey of your subject that you have located so far? Because you can't expect to remember all the peripheral ideas that occur to you as you do your research, write them down on your note cards as they come to mind. Later, when you review your cards in preparation for outlining the paper, you'll be glad for the clarifying, explanatory, or suggestive notes that you made to yourself while you were deep in the research process.

3. Recognizing a potential "note"

As this description of notes suggests, note taking is far from being a mechanical task. It is a thoughtful, even creative, act that demands your alertness and care. You may be wondering how you will recognize a "note" when you encounter one in your reading. When you are just beginning to research a topic, after all, almost everything you read about it may be new. Is everything, therefore—every page, every paragraph, every sentence—a note waiting to be jotted down? If that is so, you may be thinking, note taking will mean paraphrasing or summarizing the complete contents of every article or book you pick up.

Although there are no secret tricks that will unfailingly enable you to spot potential notes hidden among the closely packed lines of an article in the *New York Times*, note taking is, fortunately, a more selective process than the description in the previous paragraph suggests. You might keep the following general guidelines in mind as you decide what information to commit to your note cards.

1. A good note will make a clear point. If you can't understand what the author you're reading is saying, copying down a quotation from the article or a paraphrase of the text will not help you later. The notes you take should be clear enough for anyone looking over your note cards—even a person who had not read the original sources—to understand.
2. Good notes often reflect the particular attitudes or opinions of the author whom you are reading. Try to write notes that capture the essence of an author's argument, concisely restate the main point, or indicate his or her biases.
3. Good notes will present specific information—facts, places, descriptions, examples, statistics, case histories. Like all good essays, successful research papers are grounded in specific information, information that must exist on your note cards when you begin to compose your paper.

In the early stages of your work, you should expect to take many notes that you will later discard. This is an inevitable part of research work, since, as we observed earlier, it is only through the research process that you will be able to define and focus your subject clearly.

Taking notes and rethinking your original topic go hand in hand. To put it more brutally: you'll have to take many notes that you will ultimately throw away before you'll know which ones to keep.

3d Assessing your sources

Above we considered the importance of approaching note taking in a thoughtful way, isolating the key ideas in a source and finding the most accurate and most concise way to record those ideas on your note cards. Effective note taking requires another kind of reflection as well: carefully considering the quality of your sources and their appropriateness to your research project.

1. How current?

How important to your paper is *recent* information about your subject? If you are writing about historical events, you may wish to examine material published over a large span of time. A paper on the San Francisco earthquake of 1906, for example, might well draw both on contemporary accounts of the disaster and on modern assessments of its influence on subsequent city planning. In contrast, if you have chosen a current subject or one that is undergoing continual change, you will need the most up-to-date sources available. In science, politics, and medicine, for example, old information is frequently useless information.

2. How authoritative?

What can you find out about your author's qualifications to write on your subject? Begin by looking at the end of an article or on the jacket of a book for a note that cites the author's professional position or other publications. In addition, be alert for citations to your author's work in other sources, either in textual references or in footnotes. Notice whether your author's name turns up frequently in bibliographies—an indication that he or she has published widely. Finally, consider the evidence that your author uses to support his or her assertions. Is it the kind of specific and substantial information that suggests a thorough acquaintance with the subject? The better qualified the author, the more certain you can be that the information you are reading is accurate and complete.

3. How objective?

Whether or not you have been able to locate information about your author, you should watch for signs of the author's biases within his or her writing itself. Pure objectivity, of course, is rare, since every writer's perspective colors his or her handling of a subject. The question here is whether your author's biases are so strong that they may result in a distorted presentation of the subject. Is your author's work based on facts or on judgments? Does your author make questionable assumptions? Does he or she satirize or ridicule those who have taken different positions? If you detect hints of bias in your author, you will want to examine the work of a broad range of other sources as well, so that your own perspective on the subject will be as balanced as possible.

3e Assessing your subject

Use your initial note taking as a way of assessing the likelihood that the subject you've chosen will yield a successful research paper. Often, taking notes from just a few of the sources that you expect to be most promising will tell you whether your subject is going to work or not.

1. Signs of a good subject

A good subject will grow richer and more interesting as you research it. You will discover perspectives on the subject that you had not considered and will find yourself caught up in the process of discovering and synthesizing information about the topic. Your reading will suggest a number of possible directions for further research, many of which you may find intriguing.

2. Signs of a poor subject

In contrast, any of the following situations should suggest to you that your subject may be unworkable.

1. All the sources you examine make the same meager points about the subject. There's less to be learned here than you expected.
2. The sources you read suggest that the topic is far more complicated than you initially realized. You begin to feel that you will never be able to comprehend, let alone focus, your subject.
3. Your reading bores you. The subject turns out to be much less interesting than you expected.

Of course, you should give any subject a fair chance of blossoming by investigating all possible types of sources—reference works, books, magazine and journal articles, newspapers, essays in collections. Be certain, moreover, to discuss your research problems with your instructor, who may be able to help you salvage a subject that appears unworkable by suggesting a new focus for your research or specific sources for you to investigate. But don't wait until just days before your paper is due to ask your instructor for help, or for permission to look for another subject. Plan to talk with him or her at the first signs of trouble in your research.

EXERCISE 1
_____

Write a Works Cited entry in correct MLA format for each of the following sources. Note that in some cases you do not need all the information provided.

1. A review of Jane F. Gardner's book Women in Roman Law and Society, published in 1986 by the Indiana University Press in Bloomington. The review, written by Mary R. Lefkowitz, appears on pages 1185 and 1186 of volume 92 of the American Historical Review (1987), a continuously paged journal.
2. An interview with Alvin Ailey entitled Alvin Ailey Celebrates 30 Years of Dance, published in the November 1988 issue of Essence. The article begins on page 64 and continues on nonconsecutive pages later in the magazine. The interviewer is A. Peter Bailey.
3. Sheila A. Egoff's book Thursday's Child: Trends and Patterns in Contemporary Children's Literature, published in Chicago by the American Library Association. The year of publication is 1981.
4. An article entitled Of Time and Mathematics, published by Philip J. Davis in the Southern Humanities Review, volume 18, 1984. It appears on pages 193 to 202. The journal is continuously paged.
5. Frances Gray's essay The Nature of Radio Drama, in a book entitled

Radio Drama and edited by Peter Lewis. The book was published in London by Longman. The year of publication is 1981. The essay appears on pages 48 to 77.

6. Cost Estimate Jumps for Music Center Expansion, an article in the September 12, 1984, issue of the Los Angeles Times. It appears on page 1 of section VI.

7. The article Sleep in the 1983 Encyclopedia Americana. Ian Oswald wrote the article, which appears on pages 31 to 33 of volume 25. No edition is given.

8. An article in the Journal of Broadcasting by Joanne Cantor, Dean Ziemke, and Glenn G. Sparks. The title is Effect of Forewarning on Emotional Responses to a Horror Film. It appears on pages 21 to 31 of volume 28, 1984. The journal is continuously paged.

9. A two-volume book by Joseph N. Ireland entitled Records of the New York Stage from 1750 to 1860. It was originally published in 1866 and was republished in 1966 by Benjamin Blom, Inc., of New York.

10. An anonymous article on page 23 of the August 6, 1984, issue of Business Week. The title is Job Safety Becomes a Murder Issue.

11. C. A. Patrides's article Shakespeare and the Comedy beyond Comedy, published in the second number of volume 10 of the Kenyon Review, a journal that pages each issue separately. The year of publication is 1988. The article appears on pages 38 to 57.

12. A book by Charles J. Maland entitled Frank Capra. It is a volume in Twayne's Theatrical Arts Series and was published in 1980 in Boston by Twayne.

13. Charles Shapiro's afterword to Charles Dickens's novel Hard Times, published in 1961 by the Signet Classics division of New American Library in New York. The afterword is found on pages 293 to 297.

14. The article Dermatology by W. B. Shelley, found on pages 302 to 307 of The Oxford Companion to Medicine, a two-volume reference work arranged alphabetically. The editors are John Walton, Paul B. Beeson, and Ronald Bodley Scott. The book was published in Oxford by Oxford University Press in 1986.

15. A book entitled Life Insurance Companies as Financial Institutions, produced by the Life Insurance Association of America and published in 1962 by Prentice Hall in Englewood Cliffs.

EXERCISE 2

A researcher should try to summarize the major points in a source when possible, rather than copying onto a note card a host of small details. For practice in the art of summarizing, write a brief summary in your own words of each of the following passages. Try to capture both the passage's main point and its key details in no more than two sentences.

Example

Text

Babylon—the city and its empire—flourished for almost 2000 years, from about 2225 B.C. until its capture by Alexander the Great in 331 B.C. When the Greek conqueror of the world died there, Babylon could be said to have died too. But up to that time it had been the cultural capital of the civilised world; and even after its site was lost, buried under mounds of rubble, its existence was never forgotten. The very name has always had a magical sound to it. The Hebrews placed the Garden of Eden somewhere nearby. The Greeks wrote that it contained two of the Seven Wonders of the World. The Romans described it as "the greatest city the sun ever beheld." And to the early Christians "Great Babylon" was the symbol of [human] wickedness and the wrath of God. And so it was "by the waters of Babylon" that the history of the Western world could be said to have begun.

Although it seems unbelievable that a metropolis of such size and splendour should have vanished from the earth—its outer defences alone were ten miles in circumference, fifty feet high, and nearly fifty-five feet deep—the fact is that by the first century B.C. nothing remained but its walls. For Babylon had been devastated so often that by this time it was abandoned except for a few refugees who made their homes in the rubble. The royal palaces had been looted, the temples had fallen into ruins, and the greater part of the city inside the walls was overgrown with weeds.

—James Wellard, *Babylon*

Summary

By the first century B.C., little except the massive walls remained of Babylon, the most magnificent city of the world from 2225 B.C. until the fourth century B.C., a city whose reputation earned it a place in Hebrew, Greek, Roman, and early Christian myth. **[The passage's central point—expressed in this summary—is the contrast between Babylon's greatness for two thousand years and its stunning obliteration by the first century B.C.]**

1.   Despite the hype, losing weight doesn't always lead to better health. "Seesawers"—those who put on many pounds and then shed them—may nearly double their risk of heart disease, according to a study from the University of Texas School of Public Health. Those who gain little or no weight and those who put on weight but make no effort to lose it may run no additional risk of coronary disease.

        Texas researchers, who studied 400 men ages 20 to 40, theorize that seesawers who gained 10% or more of body weight after losing pounds in weight-loss programs created a sharp rise in artery-clogging cholesterol. This apparently wasn't the case with the "no-gain" and "gain-only" groups. The risk for the gain-only group: Their large, continuous gains increased the risk of fatal cancers.

        "Avoid fast-loss starvation diets," advises one of the researchers, Peggy Hamm. "If you are comfortable with your present weight, work hard at maintaining it and avoid wide fluctuations. If you're not comfortable with your weight, adjust your life-style and your eating habits so that you take the excess weight off very gradually."

                                    —"The Downside of Dieting," *Changing Times*

2.   The windmill was an inspired answer to the problem of the lack of water power, and was undoubtedly one of medieval Europe's most important inventions. Essentially an adaptation of the watermill to a new source of power, it made use of the familiar mechanism— now inverted so as to be driven by sails mounted high in the building, rather than by a waterwheel at its base. But a more fundamental alteration was also necessary. The difficulty with the windmill, and what presumably delayed its invention, was the problem of how to harness a power source that regularly changed its direction, and which would not be directed or controlled. With the watermill the water always flowed along the same channel, and at a rate the miller could vary by means of sluices; the seemingly intractable problem for the first windmill builders was to contrive a way of keeping the sails facing into the wind. The solution they came up with was to balance the windmill on a single massive upright post, so that the miller could push the whole structure around to face in whichever direction he wanted. The windspeed he could compensate for, like any sailor, by adjusting the spread of canvas on the lattice-work sails.

                                    —Richard Holt, "The Medieval Mill —A Pro-
                                    ductivity Breakthrough?" *History Today*

3.   Although dreams seem to arise unbidden, you can choose the subjects of your nighttime dramas. One technique you might try is a technique called "incubation," developed by psychologist Gayle Delaney of San Francisco. Choose a problem or question in your life, she suggests, and write down a few sentences about it. Then, just before you go to bed, compose a one-line question that sums up what you want to know, such as "Why do I fight with my spouse?" Lay the paper beside you, repeating the question over and over to yourself as you fall asleep.

When you awaken, write down everything you remember about any of your dreams. Don't reject anything as irrelevant. As Delaney says, "Dreams speak to us in symbols," so even a farfetched image may, after some wide-awake thought, be seen to bear on the incubated problem. If the technique doesn't work the first night, keep trying. Delaney reports a high success rate among her patients.

The tricky part is remembering. About the only way to capture a dream is to write it down immediately upon waking, for dreams vanish within 15 minutes. If you don't remember a dream, write down whatever is on your mind—those thoughts often come from the night's dreams and may be the first clue to retrieving them.

—"A Blueprint for Dreaming," *Newsweek*

4.   Santa Fe style isn't a reference to fashion or popularity. It's a blue sky, spiritual attitude towards life, and an abiding but quiet appreciation for a unique community culture that started in the early 1600s with sun-baked bricks of mud and straw.

Back then in 1610 when the city was officially founded on an empty mesa 7,000 feet above sea level, the rule of law came long distance from the king of Spain—with the tentative acquiescence of the local Pueblo Indians. Seven decades later, the natives revolted, and it was not until 1692 that the "city of holy faith" was reclaimed for Spanish colonialism by Don Diego de Vargas. The Republic of Mexico eventually had its heyday of authority beginning in 1821, after which Anglo traders began arriving in wagons on the old Santa Fe Trail. In 1846 during the War with Mexico, General Stephen Watts Kearny claimed Sante Fe for the Stars and Stripes.

So the city's tradition of tolerance for new faces goes way back. Today that aspect of Santa Fe's culture is perhaps its most appealing. The town is made up of many subgroups that don't mesh, yet don't clash. Among them are Hispanics who trace their local lineage back hundreds of years and world-class physicists working on nuclear re-search at the nearby Los Alamos National Laboratory. There is a huge artistic community and an army of waitresses and desk clerks. Santa Fe being the capital city, its state-government contingent numbers in the thousands. And there's a shockingly large collection of the world's wealthiest individuals who keep very much to themselves.

This is an impossible mix. But the suspension holds—even after they stirred in the New Agers with their vegetarian dream rolfing and herbal acu-massage therapy, and the Sikhs with their turbans and beards. Santa Fe is open to almost all ways of thinking, and that makes for a far more interesting, cosmopolitan city than its size and location would ordinarily suggest.

> —Paul Young, "Santa Fe Style: Impossible
> Cosmopolitan Mix," *American West*

4 Composing the Research Paper

Perhaps the most important advice to keep in mind as you organize and write your paper is that the research paper, though it may be longer than other essays you have written, is more similar to than different from a typical expository essay, and its success will depend largely on the same principles of effective writing that you have studied in other contexts. If you have learned how to formulate a thesis and introduction, how to write clearly structured paragraphs, how to use specific diction and development effectively, how to ensure coherence and maintain consistency of tone, then you should be able to write a good research paper.

There is no denying, however, that the matter of integrating other people's ideas and words with your own text complicates the task of composing a research paper. Accordingly, the section below presents some guidelines to follow as you organize your paper, and the following two sections deal specifically with incorporating information from your sources into the paper. This chapter ends by considering some important matters of format for your final draft.

4a Organizing and writing a research paper

The more you learn about your subject from note taking, the more you may feel that you will never be able to stop examining sources without the risk of missing some potentially important new piece of information. Strictly speaking, of course, that's true. But the realities of research—whether in college or in professional life—dictate that you must at some point call a halt to your research and begin shaping into a coherent whole the material that you have collected.

1.   Know when to stop taking notes

How will you know when you've collected enough information and can begin writing your paper? It's difficult to be certain that you've done enough research, but you might expect your work to lead to this point in stages something like the following.

Examine your major sources

First, take notes from all of your major sources, that is, all of those that you initially expected to be important sources of information on your topic, either because their titles seemed particularly promising or because you had already skimmed through them. As we noted at the end of the preceding chapter, you should complete this stage of the research process with a reasonably sure sense that your subject is in some way going to provide the basis for a successful paper.

Look for connections among your notes

Once you move beyond your list of major sources and start examining others, you will probably discover a number of the same topics surfacing again and again, and you will begin to see connections among your note cards for the first time. Source Y, for example, has an opinion different from source X's; source B confirms a point made by source A. Recognizing such connections is a good sign that you are mastering your subject. This is usually the point at which you will be able to define a more precise direction for your paper and your additional research. You will have become familiar enough with your subject to identify those aspects of it that seem most worth investigating.

Think about what your research proves

At about this point, you will no doubt realize that you have developed ideas of your own about your subject, based on the reading and note taking you have done. The best researchers, after all, are less interested in mere piles of accumulated data than in ways of using the data they have collected to support their own observations and ideas.

Once you are able to see beyond your separate notes to the ways in which those notes can be used to substantiate a larger argument of your own, a sense of the completeness of your work may begin to grow upon you. You may gradually begin to develop a vague mental outline of some of the key ideas you think your paper should cover. When you reach this point, it may be time to retire from the library—for a while, at least—and have a try at writing your paper.

2. Organize your notes

The first stage in writing your paper is reviewing and sorting out all of the notes you have taken, collecting together notes from different sources that explain, comment on, or give evidence for the same specific points. If you have put your notes on separate cards or slips of paper, you will find this easy to do.

As you read each note card, decide which aspect of your subject it pertains to, and group it with others that address the same issue. Don't be surprised if you have a large "miscellaneous" category made up of notes whose value seems questionable; many of your early note cards may indeed be no longer important, now that you have more clearly focused your subject. Realize, however, that although sorting out your note cards will help you define the main issues to concentrate on in your paper, it may also reveal points that need further research. Some additional trips to the library in search of specific pieces of information may still be necessary before your paper is finished.

Some writers, in sorting out their note cards, attach a "comment card" to each note card, briefly indicating the way they expect to use the note in the paper. Later, when they have begun writing, they can easily expand the comment card into a sentence or two that establishes a clear context for the material on the note cards. This practice helps to guarantee that the finished paper will not be a mere splicing together of facts or quotations; instead, the notes will function as part of a larger argument created by the researcher.

3. Compose a tentative outline

Few writers can progress beyond this point in composing a long paper without making at least an informal outline. The piles of note cards before you will help. Each of the large piles may be one of the main points in your paper, a main heading in your outline. Within each pile you will find notes that will make up the subpoints to be covered. With your usable notes organized in groups before you, sketch out an outline of your paper on a separate sheet of paper, including all the subpoints that you have notes to support. Some writers like to mark their note cards to correspond with the points in their written outline, so that they will know just which cards to pick up as they compose the paper.

4. Segment your writing

Even a researcher who begins writing with a firm grasp of his or her subject and a clear conception of the form that he or she wants the final research paper to take may sometimes feel overwhelmed by the amount of material to be assimilated into the paper. For that reason, many researchers view their papers in segments, and they approach the task of writing by thinking about and working on only one segment at a time. For example, you might set as the goal of your first composing session drafting only the introduction to your paper—the opening paragraph or paragraphs that will provide the reader with necessary background on your subject and introduce the paper's thesis. If you have formulated a tentative outline, make drafting just one new section of the outline the objective of each successive composing session. Don't feel that you have to compose the paper's parts sequentially; if you get stuck while writing one segment, leave it temporarily and work on a different one instead.

As in all writing, your goal is to put down on paper a draft, not a final polished essay. Write in any way that will help you move along quickly, whether that means using a soft pencil, a ballpoint pen, a typewriter, or a word processor. Skip lines if you write by hand, so that you will have room for later additions and changes.

In **4c** below, we will consider ways of incorporating quotation and paraphrasing into your paper. But it is appropriate here to point out that you shouldn't take the time to copy into your draft quotations that you intend to use in your text. Instead, simply clip the note card with the quotation on it to the appropriate page of the draft. The time to worry about smoothly incorporating such material into your text will come later, as you revise.

5. Leave time for rethinking and revising

When you do begin revising, you should probably be prepared to make more changes than you might have made in other papers you have written. The length of a research paper and the number of different materials on which it is based open up a variety of possibilities for its organization, and you need to be ready to reassemble your material in several ways before you find a satisfactory arrangement. Transitional words, phrases, and sentences will be more important than ever as you attempt to link together smoothly the information gathered from your various sources and your own observations and conclusions.

Be prepared, too, for the possibility that you will have to return to the library to check a source or page number, to make sense of a confusing but important note card, or even to do some additional research. For these reasons, plan to leave enough time to write your earliest draft in several sittings, to put it away for a day or two (or at least overnight), and then to return to it fresh for thorough revision. A research paper is a complex project, and you should not expect to be able to dash off a draft one evening, patch it up the next, and hand it in the following morning. Apart from matters of composition— formidable enough in a paper of this length—you will need time to double-check the accuracy of your citations, type up the paper in the correct format, and proofread carefully. Leave yourself enough time to assemble a paper worthy of the weeks of research you have completed.

4b Avoiding plagiarism

Although the research paper is similar in many respects to the other writing you have done, it presents you with at least one major new task: accurately citing the sources of your research. If you fail to distinguish between your own words and thoughts and those of your sources, you mislead your reader into assuming that everything in the paper is your own work. Passing off the language or ideas of someone else as your own is a serious violation known as **plagiarism.**

In **4c** we will consider the proper format for citing sources in your paper. Before we do that, however, we need to look more closely at the concept of plagiarism itself, particularly as it pertains to using quotation and paraphrase in a research paper. Those are the two basic situations in which you must cite your sources in order to avoid plagiarizing, and we will examine them separately.

1. Quoting accurately

You must enclose every direct quotation in quotation marks, and you must cite its source in the paper. This rule is easy enough to understand. If you did not enclose in quotation marks the direct quotations that you take from your sources, your reader would have no way of knowing which words were yours and which were your sources'. And once you do use quotation marks to set off these phrases or sentences, your reader's natural question will be, "Who wrote this?" Your citation of the source answers that question.

A quotation must present the words of your source exactly as they appear in the original text unless you use ellipsis marks or brackets to indicate that you have made changes in the text. Be careful not to distort the meaning of the original text by omitting key words or by using the quoted passage in a sense not intended by the original writer. Consider the following examples.

Source

> In a given area the plague accomplished its kill within four to six months and then faded, except in the larger cities, where, rooting into the close-quartered population, it abated during the winter, only to reappear in spring and rage for another six months.
>
> —Barbara W. Tuchman, *A Distant Mirror: The Calamitous 14th Century* (New York: Knopf, 1978) 93.

Inaccurate use of quotation

In fourteenth-century cities, the plague "rooted into the close population during the winter, only to reappear in spring and rage for another six months" (Tuchman 93).

[The quoted passage in this sentence resembles Tuchman's, but it is not a word-for-word reproduction of her text, and it is therefore unacceptable. This writer has changed the word *rooting* to "rooted," and has omitted the words *quartered* and *it abated*.]

Inaccurate use of quotation

According to Barbara Tuchman, the great plague of the fourteenth century lasted only "four to six months and then faded" (93).

[This writer has quoted Tuchman's words accurately but has radically distorted her meaning by ignoring the rest of her sentence, where she refers to the plague's cyclical return in the cities, year after year.]

Accurate use of quotation

In medieval cities, according to Barbara Tuchman, the plague "abated during the winter" but typically "[reappeared] in spring and [raged] for another six months" (93).

[To make Tuchman's words fit the structure of his sentence, this writer had to change the original text's *reappear* and *rage* to *reappeared* and *raged*; he indicated those changes in an acceptable way, by putting the substituted words in brackets. Otherwise, the quoted passages are faithful to the original.]

2. Paraphrasing accurately

You must cite the source of every paraphrased idea unless that idea would be considered common knowledge. To explain this documentation rule, we need to consider separately its two key terms, **paraphrase** and **common knowledge.**

Paraphrasing

To paraphrase an idea means to change the words in which it is expressed without materially altering its meaning. Many writers have difficulty grasping the precise point at which the wording of a quotation has been sufficiently altered to constitute an acceptable paraphrase. *In general, several words in succession taken from another source may be said to constitute direct quotation.* Thus you cannot turn a quotation into an acceptable sentence of your own simply by changing a few words in the original. Consider the following examples, based on the same excerpt from Barbara Tuchman that we used above.

Unacceptable paraphrase

> In a specific area the plague killed its victims in
>
> four to six months and then receded, except in big
>
> cities, where it declined in the winter, only to reap-
>
> pear in spring and flourish for another six months
>
> (Tuchman 93).

[This writer has merely substituted a few words of his own for words in the source. The structure of the sentence, however, is Tuchman's. The result is plagiarism.]

Unacceptable paraphrase

> The plague accomplished its kill within four to six
>
> months in most places, but in the cities it abated
>
> during the winter and would rage again in the spring
>
> (Tuchman 93).

[The structure of this writer's sentence is original, but she has used several phrases taken directly from Tuchman: *accomplished its kill within four to six months, abated during the winter.* Borrowing such phrases without enclosing them in quotation marks makes the writer guilty of plagiarism. Just the word *rage* as used here would constitute plagiarism in most readers' eyes, even though it is not part of a longer phrase taken from Tuchman, because it is such a distinctive verb in Tuchman's original sentence.]

Acceptable paraphrase

In the crowded cities, the plague never completely disappeared; though relatively dormant in the winter, it returned in full force when the weather turned warm again (Tuchman 93).

[This writer has captured the exact meaning of Tuchman's passage, but in a sentence that is original in structure and diction. The only major words taken from Tuchman are *cities, plague,* and *winter;* such duplication is acceptable, since it would be impossible to find synonyms for these basic terms.]

Common knowledge

As shown above, even a quotation converted into acceptable paraphrase must have its source cited in your paper unless it falls into a category often referred to as "common knowledge." What does common knowledge mean?

In practice, writers often find it simply impossible to give sources for everything they write. Where, for instance, did these rules for avoiding plagiarism come from? It would be difficult to say, since people have talked and written about the concept of plagiarism for several centuries at least. Our sense of what the term means in the 1990s is a good example of common knowledge, part of our understanding for which we have no single identifiable source.

If you are unsure whether an idea you encounter in your research qualifies as common knowledge, you might keep in mind the following two-step test. An idea is common knowledge and its source need not be cited *only* if

1. you found it repeated in many sources, rather than stated in just one; or
2. you believe it would be familiar to an average educated person, even one who had not researched the subject (a person, for example, like one of your classmates).

For example, the fact that the Olympic games originated in Greece would not need citation, since it fulfills both of the conditions above (it is information that would be found in many books and articles on the Olympics, *and* it is a fact familiar to most people). Nor would the fact that the modern Olympic games were begun in 1896 require citation; although that fact fails the second condition (most people you asked would probably not be able to give you this date), it passes the first (anyone doing research on the Olympics would repeatedly encounter the date in a variety of sources).

In contrast, a single author's opinion about the propaganda value of the 1936 Berlin Olympics in Nazi Germany would probably need a citation, even if the opinion were acceptably paraphrased. Such a statement would not meet either of the conditions above. As a specific writer's opinion, it would appear only in a single source (though if you found a great many writers who shared this opinion, it would then qualify as common knowledge after all). And as the statement of a presumed authority on the Olympics, it would not be information that we could expect others who had not studied the subject to know.

4c   Citing sources

Above we examined the situations in which you must indicate the sources of the material—whether quoted or paraphrased—that you have used in writing your research paper. In this section, we turn to the method of making such citations in the text of your paper.

The system of documentation adopted by the Modern Language Association of America in 1984 eliminates the elaborate footnotes used for years by both students and scholars. The simplicity of this new system and the academic prestige of its proponent, the MLA, have brought it into widespread use, particularly in the humanities. Keep in mind, however, that preferred methods of documentation vary arbitrarily from discipline to discipline. Chapters **6** and **7** present two other widely used forms of documentation, the system of parenthetical citation prescribed by the American Psychological Association and the system of endnote documentation formerly advocated by the MLA. Still other methods of documentation exist as well. The best approach for you to adopt is simply to follow closely whatever model your instructor suggests.

The MLA system reduces documentation to two components. First, at the end of each passage whose source must be noted, the last name of the author and the page or pages on which the material is found are inserted in parentheses:

```
(Alexander 197-98)
```

At the end of the paper, on a separate sheet with the heading "Works Cited," a complete bibliographic entry is provided for each of the sources cited in the text (see the sample Works Cited list on page 111). These entries, which follow the forms described in **3b**, are arranged alphabetically according to the last names of the authors:

```
Alexander, Edwin P.  On the Main Line: The Pennsylva-

    nia Railroad in the 19th Century.  New York:

    Potter, 1971.
```

If you properly filled out a bibliography card for each of your sources as you took notes, you will be able to alphabetize the cards for the sources you used and copy your Works Cited entries directly from them.

The examples below illustrate this method of citing sources and some ways of smoothly incorporating quoted and paraphrased material into your text.

1. Quotations

Typically, the parenthetical citation in a text comes *after* the quotation marks that close a quotation but *before* the sentence's end punctuation:

Parenthetical citation in text

The definitive biography of Mahatma Gandhi remains

to be written. As one Gandhi scholar has explained,

"Multivolume works written by Gandhi's former col-

leagues and published in India are comprehensive in

scope, but their objectivity suffers from the au-

thors' reverent regard for their subject" (Juer-

gensmeyer 294).

Citation in works cited

Juergensmeyer, Mark. "The Gandhi Revival—A Review

Article." Journal of Asian Studies 43 (1984):

293-98.

What follows are some variations on this basic method of documenting quotations.

Setting off a long quotation

A quotation of more than four lines is set off from the text and indented ten spaces from the left margin. Such a quotation is usually introduced with a colon unless it begins in the middle of a sentence that grammatically continues the sentence that introduces it. The parenthetical citation is placed *after* the end punctuation.

Parenthetical citation in text

One editor suggests that photographers trying to publish their work should aim to surpass—not just
equal—the photographs they see in print:

> Editors know where they can get pictures
> like the ones they've already published.
> If you want to get noticed, you have to take
> pictures better than those. This is espe-
> cially true if you are looking for assign-
> ments rather than to sell existing pic-
> tures. Why take a chance on a new
> photographer who will come up with no bet-
> ter than what you already have, an editor
> might reason? (Scully 33)

Citation in works cited

Scully, Judith. "Seeing Pictures." Modern Photography May 1984: 28–33.

Incorporating the author's name into the text

You can often fit quotations into your text smoothly by introducing the author's name before the quotation or by placing it at
some point in the middle of the quotation. In such cases, only the
page number of the source needs to appear in the parenthetical citation.
The following examples illustrate both of these techniques:

Parenthetical citation in text

The English, notes Richard Altick, are obsessed by
love for their dogs: "Walking dogs is a ritual that

proceeds independently of weather, cataclysms, and the movements of the planets; they are led or carried everywhere, into department stores, fishmongers', greengrocers', buses, trains" (286).

Citation in works cited

Altick, Richard D. <u>To Be in England</u>. New York: Norton, 1969.

Parenthetical citation in text

"After watching a lot of music videos," Holly Brubach observes, "it's hard to escape the conclusions that no one has the nerve to say no to a rock-and-roll star and that most videos would be better if someone did" (102).

Citation in works cited

Brubach, Holly. "Rock-and-Roll Vaudeville." <u>Atlantic</u> July 1984: 99-102.

Citing a work by more than one author

When two or three persons wrote the material that you wish to quote, include the names of all. Follow the same order in which the names are printed in the original source:

Parenthetical citation in text

Selvin and Wilson argue that "a concern for effective writing is not a trivial elevation of form over content. Good writing is a condition, slowly achieved, of . . . being what one means to be" (207).

Citation in works cited

```
Selvin, Hanan C., and Everett K. Wilson. "On Sharp-
     ening Sociologists' Prose." Sociological
     Quarterly 25 (1984): 205-22.
```

When your source is a work by more than three authors, give the name only of the first in your parenthetical text citation, followed by the abbreviation *et al.* (Latin for "and others") not underlined. For example:

```
(Leventhal et al. 54)
```

Citing an anonymous work

If the author of the material you are quoting is not given, use the title, or a shortened form of the title, in your parenthetical text citation. Place the titles of articles in quotation marks; underline the titles of books. Remember that, whenever you quote, you may use part of an author's sentence rather than the whole, as long as the section you have chosen fits into the syntax of your own sentence and does not misrepresent the author's original meaning:

Parenthetical citation in text

```
Environmentalists protested that a recent study of
the plan to spray herbicides on marijuana "systemati-
cally underestimated the possibility of damage from
such spraying and exaggerated the benefits to be
achieved by a spraying program" ("Marijuana Spray-
ing" 14).
```

Citation in works cited

```
"Marijuana Spraying Opposed." New York Times 22
     Aug. 1984: 14.
```

In the case of a one-page article like that above, the page number may be omitted in the text citation.

Citing a multivolume work

The parenthetical text citation to a work in more than one volume includes the volume number and a colon before the page citation:

Parenthetical citation in text

The medieval manor house dominated nearby cottages

"not only because it was better built, but above all

because it was almost invariably designed for de-

fence" (Bloch 2: 300).

Citation in works cited

Bloch, Marc. Feudal Society. Trans. L. A. Manyon.

2 vols. Chicago: U of Chicago P, 1961.

Citing two works by the same author

If your list of Works Cited includes more than one work by the same author, your parenthetical text citations to this author must indicate which work you are referring to. In such cases, add a shortened version of the relevant title. In the list of Works Cited, substitute three hyphens and a period for the author's name in the second citation.

Parenthetical citation in text

"Of America's eastern rivers," writes one historian,

"none was longer or potentially more important than

the one the Indians accurately described as the

'Long-reach River'—Susquehanna" (Hanlon, Wyoming

Valley 17).

Citations in works cited

Hanlon, Edward F. The Wyoming Valley: An American

Portrait. Woodland Hills: Windsor, 1983.

———. "Urban-Rural Cooperation and Conflict in the

Congress: The Breakdown of the New Deal Coali-

tion, 1933-1938." Diss. Georgetown U, 1967.

2. Paraphrases

A successful research paper is more than a string of quotations. Although a strategically placed quotation can help to focus a paragraph or emphasize a point, an extended series of quotations in a research paper often creates the impression of disjointedness and confusion. Look instead for opportunities to express in your own words the ideas that you have discovered during your research.

As the following examples illustrate, the rules described above for acknowledging the sources of quotations also apply to paraphrased material.

Parenthetical citation in text (author's name in parenthetical citation)

The steadily growing role of television in politics

has helped to shift attention away from the politi-

cians' stands on issues to the way they appear before

the camera (Meyrowitz 51).

Citation in works cited

Meyrowitz, Joshua. "Politics in the Video Eye: Where

Have All the Heroes Gone?" Psychology Today

July 1984: 46-51.

Parenthetical citation in text (author's name incorporated into text)

One effect of the microscope's development in the late 1600s, Paul Fussell points out, was to change attitudes toward insects. Whereas people in the seventeenth century had considered insects innocuous creatures, eighteenth-century men and women, exposed for the first time to drawings of magnified insect bodies, regarded them as hideous and contemptible (235-36).

Citation in works cited

Fussell, Paul. The Rhetorical World of Augustan Humanism: Ethics and Imagery from Swift to Burke. London: Oxford UP, 1965.

Parenthetical citation in text (source with two authors)

Computers may be dominating the modern office, but architects are beginning to counter this technological takeover by designing comfortable and inviting office interiors (Davies and Malone 73).

Citation in works cited

Davies, Douglas, and Maggie Malone. "Offices of the Future." Newsweek 14 May 1984: 72+.

Parenthetical citation in text (anonymous source)

Some airport delays, it appears, can be blamed on government deregulation of the airlines. On at least

one weekday at Kennedy International Airport, for
example, airlines have now scheduled over sixty ar-
rivals between four and five o'clock, even though
the airport can accommodate only forty-nine landings
each hour ("Not Quite Ready" 25).

Citation in works cited

"Not Quite Ready When You Are." Time 9 July 1984:
25.

3. Content notes

Although footnotes have been eliminated from the citing of
sources in the MLA system of documentation, they may still be used
to add supplementary information to the text of a research paper.
Such notes, often referred to as **content notes,** are indicated in the
text with consecutive superscript numerals and are placed either at
the bottom of the appropriate page or together on a separate sheet,
with the heading "Notes," inserted after the text of the paper and
before the Works Cited page. If you collect your notes together on a
separate sheet, as most instructors prefer, double-space between and
within the notes. Indent the first line of each note five spaces.

Content notes offer a convenient means of including explanatory
material or referring the reader to additional sources of information:

Text with superscript

The art of biographical writing in nineteenth-century England has generally been undervalued,[1] with
the result that modern readers tend to regard Victo-
rian biographies with a certain condescension and
smugness.

Note

   [1] A few recent authors, however, have recognized the artistic merit of at least some nineteenth-
century biographical writing. For useful readings
of several major biographies of the period, see
Gwiasda and Reed.

The full publication information for sources mentioned in notes is supplied in the Works Cited list:

Citations in works cited

Gwiasda, Karl E. "The Boswell Biographers: A Study
        of 'Life and Letters' Writing in the Victorian
        Period." Diss. Northwestern U, 1969.
Reed, Joseph W., Jr. English Biography in the Early
        Nineteenth Century, 1801-1838. New Haven:
        Yale UP, 1966.

4d   Formatting the research paper

   The physical appearance of a research paper makes its own contribution to the paper's effectiveness. A meticulously prepared paper naturally inclines the reader to expect content of equal quality. Haphazard typing, by contrast, can undercut the authority of even the best research and writing by giving a reader the impression of hasty and careless work. Proper format, therefore, is more than a superficial concern.
   The format guidelines below are based on those suggested by the Modern Language Association. Your instructor may give you supplementary or alternative instructions to follow.

1. Paper

Using a typewriter or computer printer with a fresh ribbon, type or print out your research paper on standard 8½-by-11-inch white bond. Do not use onionskin paper, which is hard to read, or erasable typing paper, which easily smears. For convenient reading, most instructors prefer that the pages of a research paper be held together with a paper clip rather than stapled or fastened in a folder.

2. Spacing and margins

Double-space everything in your paper—text, long quotations, notes, and Works Cited list. Double-space as well between page headings (such as "Works Cited") and the first line of text on the page.

Leave a one-inch margin on the top, bottom, and sides of each page. Page headings such as "Notes" and "Works Cited" are centered just within this margin, one inch from the top of the page. Page numbers are placed outside the top margin, one-half inch from the top of the page and one inch from the right side of the page. Number all pages, including the first. You should not use punctuation or abbreviations such as p. with page numbers; however, to guard against pages becoming separated and misplaced, you may precede the number on the top of each page with your last name: Smith 1, Smith 2, and so on.

3. Title page

Do not include a separate title page unless your instructor specifically requests it. Instead, on four separate double-spaced lines in the upper left corner of the first page, type your name, the name of your instructor, the course number, and the date. Double-space, center the title of your paper, and double-space to begin the text of the paper. Double-space between lines of your title if it runs onto a second line. (See the sample title page on page 95.)

(See the sample title page on page 95.)

EXERCISE 1

Treat each of the passages below as if it were to become part of a research paper you are writing. In each case, compose the following:

1. A few sentences of your own incorporating an acceptable paraphrase of one or more of the ideas in the passage.
2. A few sentences of your own incorporating a quotation taken from the passage. (Remember that if you quote only part of a sentence, the phrase or clause that you quote must fit into the syntax of your sentence.)
3. A citation of the source in proper form for a Works Cited list.

Remember to include appropriate parenthetical text citations in your sentences for the first two items above.

1. Los Angeles, one might reasonably guess, is the most prodigious user of water in the state of California, if not the entire world. At least 12 million people inhabit the metropolitan region, a sightless sprawl that has filled a basin twice the size of Luxembourg and is spilling into the ultramontane deserts beyond. The climate is semi-arid to emphatically dry, although many people, including Anglenos, seem surprised when you point this out, because enough water comes in by aqueduct each day (about two billion gallons) to have transformed this former stubbly grassland and alkali waste into an ersatz Miami, six times as large. Los Angeles now diverts the entire flow of the Owens River, one of the largest of the eastern Sierra Nevada streams; it appropriates a substantial share of the Colorado River, the largest by far in the American Southwest; it siphons off about a third of the flow of the Feather River, one of the biggest in the state, through an aqueduct 445 miles long. The few meager streams in and around the basin have long since been sucked dry.

    In Los Angeles, even after months of habitual drought (southern California is virtually rainless from April through November), the fastidiously manicured lawns remain green. The swimming pools remain filled, eight million cars well washed. There are verdant cemeteries for humans and their pets. The Palm Springs Chamber of Commerce boasts of more than 100 golf courses, shining like green lakes in that desiccated landscape, where it rains about four inches in a typical year. Los Angeles is a palpable mirage, a vast outdoor Disneyland, the Babylon and Ur of the desert empire that is the American West.
    [The opening two paragraphs of an article in the bimonthly magazine Greenpeace. The title of the article is The Emerald Desert; the author is Marc Reisner; the article appears on pages 6 to 10 of the July-August 1989 issue.]

2. What were the Romans like at that time—at the beginning of contact with the older Greeks in the middle of the third century B.C.? They were a small group of a few hundred thousand souls, one group of several that had emerged from barbarous central Europe and pushed their way into Italy in search for land, and they had long plodded on in silence at the dull task of making the soil provide food. For a while they had been subdued by the Etruscans, but taught by their conquerors to use arms in strong masses, they had applied this lesson by driving off their oppressors and re-establishing their old independent town meetings, returning again to the tilling of the soil. A prolific and puritanic folk with a strict social morality, they outgrew their boundaries and began to expand. In the contests that resulted the Romans came off the victors. In [page break] organizing the adjacent tribes into a federal union they revealed a peculiar liberalism—unmatched anywhere among the barbarians of that day—by abstaining from the exaction of tribute; they also betrayed an imagination of high quality in the invention of cooperative leagues, and unusual capacity for legal logic in the shaping of municipal and civic forms.

   [A passage on pages 9 and 10 (note the page break indicated in this excerpt) in Tenney Frank's book Life and Literature in the Roman Republic, originally published in 1930 as volume seven of the Sather Classical Lectures, republished in 1965 by the University of California Press at Berkeley.]

3. In a Boston business district that lately has been overwhelmed by glass and metal office towers, oddly shaped hotels, and an abundance of trendy shops, a few vestiges of the old "Hub City" remain. Paul Revere's house still stands in a neighborhood that is fighting off condominium developers. Faneuil Hall, a revolutionary war meetinghouse, is the centerpiece of a burgeoning plaza full of shops and restaurants. Baseballs still fly over the left-field wall at Fenway Park, one of the last surviving stadiums that knew Babe Ruth. And then there's South Station.

   Once South Station dominated its neighborhood in Dewey Square; now it lays in the shadow of several of those new office towers. But at age 90, South Station is nearing the end of a major facelift that will ensure its status as a Boston landmark into the next century. At the same time, South Station remains one of the busiest stations on Amtrak's busiest route, the Northeast Corridor, of which it is the northern anchor.

[From page 38 of an article by Tom Nelligan in Trains, a monthly magazine. The article, entitled Boston South Station Revival, runs from page 38 to page 42 in the June 1989 issue.]

4. In the second half of the seventeenth century, Holland, a term used to describe the seven United Provinces of the Northern Netherlands, was at the peak of its world power and prestige. With its dense, teeming population of two million hard-working Dutchmen crowded into a tiny area, Holland was by far the richest, most urbanized, most cosmopolitan state in Europe. Not surprisingly, the prosperity of this small state was a source of wonder and envy to its neighbors, and often this envy turned to greed. On such occasions, the Dutch drew on certain national characteristics to defend themselves. They were valiant, obstinate and resourceful, and when they fought—first against the Spaniards, then against the English and finally against the French—they fought in a way which was practical and, at the same time, desperately and sublimely heroic.

[Passage is on page 178 of Peter the Great: His Life and World, by Robert K. Massie, published in 1981 in New York by Ballantine Books. The book was first published by Alfred A. Knopf in 1980.]

5. Pity the Pilgrims, who stepped ashore to confront a wall of forest and a cruel joke beneath the trees. New England stands on granite. Except for the silted beaver meadows and alluvial valleys like the Connecticut, the glaciers left the colonists only a thin mantle of hilly, stony soil. The Southeast also was of mineral-poor rock, and it had weathered too long in the rain. Save for the river deltas and the limestone valleys, its old soils were largely pooped out before the first ax rang in the forest.

[Passage is on page 376 of an article by Boyd Gibbons on pages 350 to 388 of National Geographic, September, 1984. The title of the article is Do We Treat Our Soil Like Dirt?]

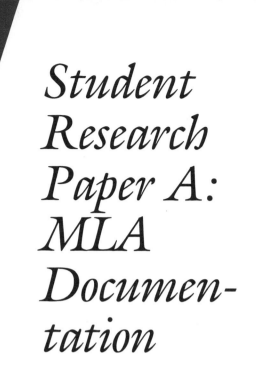

5 Student Research Paper A: MLA Documentation

Suzanne Conlon's research paper, "Anne Bradstreet's Homespun Cloth: The First American Poems," may be a bit shorter than the paper you are working on, but it illustrates well the principles of research discussed in the last four chapters.

First, Conlon positions and develops her thesis very effectively. It comes at the end of two paragraphs of introduction, paragraphs that give even the reader who knows nothing about Bradstreet and her times enough information to follow the paper's argument. In the rest of the paper, Conlon develops that argument—that Bradstreet's poetry reflects her human rebelliousness as well as her Puritan submissiveness—by interweaving her own analyses of key poems with the observations of other critics.

This deft and unobtrusive use of sources is in fact one of the paper's main strengths. The facts and brief quotations that Conlon inserts here and there add texture to her analysis without overshadowing her own presence in the paper. The paper never becomes a mere summary of other people's ideas; instead, it remains sharply analytical, punctuated by Conlon's subtle reminders of the way in which the points she is making advance her thesis.

For the origin of Conlon's title, see her analysis of Bradstreet's poem "The Author to Her Book" in the fourth paragraph of the paper.

Conlon has quoted rather than paraphrased Rich's words because they offer an especially vivid impression of the Massachusetts Bay Colony. The themes of desolation and hardship that the quotation introduces will be important to Conlon's analysis of Bradstreet's poetry.

Compare Conlon's excerpt from Bradstreet's letter to her children with the original text:

> After a short time I changed my condition and was married, and came into this country, where I found a new world and new manners, at which my heart rose. But after I was convinced it was the way of God, I submitted to it and joined to the church at Boston.

Conlon has selected only the passage in these sentences that directly relates to Bradstreet's reactions to the New World and has inserted in brackets the words *in revolt* to clarify the intended meaning in Bradstreet's somewhat ambiguously worded sentence. The ellipses at the end of the quotation indicate the omission of the final words of the original text. The superscript *1*, raised a half-line, refers the reader to the content note after the last page of the paper.

1/2"
1

1"

Suzanne E. Conlon

Professor Les Perelman

English 100

February 22, 1990

Anne Bradstreet's Homespun Cloth:

The First American Poems

In 1630 a young Englishwoman sailed for the New World with her husband and parents aboard the <u>Arbella</u>, the flagship of the Winthrop fleet carrying Puritan settlers from Southampton to the Massachusetts Bay Colony (White 103). The voyage was rough and uncomfortable, and the landing was not quite the relief that the eighteen-year-old bride had expected; she had been brought, in Adrienne Rich's words, to "the wild coast of Massachusetts Bay, the blazing heat of an American June, the half-dying, famine-ridden frontier village of Salem, clinging to the edge of an incalculable land-mass" (ix). Forty years later Bradstreet was to write in a letter to her children that she "found a new world and new manners, at which my heart rose [in revolt]. But after I was convinced it was the way of God, I submitted to it . . ." ("To My Dear Children").[1]

The long Richardson quotation has been cut down by the two omissions indicated with ellipses. The omitted words are irrelevant to Conlon's point here. Note that a quotation with ellipses must make grammatical and logical sense without the omitted words.

The factual information about the publication of Bradstreet's book is available in many sources and may therefore be considered common knowledge. It does not need specific documentation.

2

The conflict between revulsion and submission
that Bradstreet expresses in these lines can be
traced to her Puritan background. As one scholar explains, "The Puritan was always trying to achieve a
balance between this world and the next. . . . One
could not safely turn one's back on this world, for
the simple reason that God has made it and found it
good; yet one could not rely upon . . . an earthly
life which was, at last, insubstantial" (Richardson
317-18). Anne Bradstreet's dilemma involved a similar conflict between opposite impulses. Instead of
loving the New World, she at first hated the harsh
life it imposed on colonists, but this feeling went
against her conviction that God's will demanded her
to stay there and submit. Eventually she managed to
strike her own balance: despite periods of doubt and
depression, she bore and raised eight children in
the wilderness near Andover, and in intervals stolen
from her scanty leisure time she wrote five long
didactic poems. The poems had been collected in manuscript as a present for her father, Thomas Dudley,
and they were not meant to be published. But her
brother-in-law took the manuscript with him on a
journey to England and had it printed, as a surprise,

Conlon has used her first two paragraphs to establish the background needed for an understanding of Bradstreet—her arrival in America, her conflicting attitudes toward the New World, the essential elements of her Puritan background, and the origins of her book. All of these points converge in Conlon's thesis at the end of paragraph 2—that Bradstreet's poetry combines rebelliousness and submission in an American variation of the Puritan dilemma.

Conlon has skillfully fitted the lines of verse that she quotes into the grammatical structure of her sentence. Compare her excerpt with the complete stanza in Bradstreet's poem:

> I am obnoxious to each carping tongue
> Who says my hand a needle better fits,
> A poet's pen all scorn I should thus wrong,
> For such despite they cast on female wits:
> If what I do prove well, it won't advance,
> They'll say it's stol'n, or else it was by chance.

In Conlon's text, a slash (/) indicates the line division, and her citation provides the title of the poem and the lines she has quoted. (See Conlon's content note after the last page of the paper.)

Conlon quotes rather than paraphrases Cotton Mather because his words vividly illustrate the Puritans' distaste for poetry. The citation "qtd. in Hoffman 253" indicates that Mather's words are directly *quoted* by Hoffman on page 253 of his book. Compare with "Hoffman 253," which would indicate that the words were Hoffman's own.

3

under the title The Tenth Muse, Lately Sprung Up in
America. In its combination of human rebelliousness
and spiritual submission, Anne Bradstreet's poetry
represents an American variation of the "Puritan dilemma" (Miller and Johnson 2: 287) as it was experienced by a sensitive, cultivated, and pious woman
of early New England.

A good Puritan woman was supposed to base her
life on submission to God and to subordinate her own
interests to the welfare of her father, husband, and
family. Anne Bradstreet was fully aware of "each
carping tongue/Who says my hand a needle better fits"
("The Prologue" 27-28). Such critics held that it
was an aberration for a woman to write at all. It
was even more unseemly, if not actually sinful, for
a Puritan woman to write poetry. To the Puritan mind,
poetry represented attachment to the things of this
world: to words rather than to the dogma that words
were meant to communicate, to the natural world
rather than to the Heavenly Kingdom, to loved ones
rather than to God. Cotton Mather, the great Puritan
preacher, announced magisterially that poets were
"the most numerous as well as the most venomous authors" in the Devil's Library on earth (qtd. in Hoff-

Anne Bradstreet's poem "The Author to Her Book" is reprinted below. Note that Conlon has selected from it just those phrases she needs and has fitted them smoothly into her own sentence structure to create a concise and effective summary.

The Author to Her Book

Thou ill-formed offspring of my feeble brain,
Who after birth didst by my side remain,
Till snatched from thence by friends, less wise than true,
Who thee abroad, exposed to public view,
Made thee in rags, halting to th' press to trudge,
Where errors were not lessened (all may judge).
At thy return my blushing was not small,
My rambling brat (in print) should mother call,
I cast thee by as one unfit for light,
Thy visage was so irksome in my sight;
Yet being mine own, at length affection would
Thy blemishes amend, if so I could:
I washed thy face, but more defects I saw,
And rubbing off a spot still made a flaw.
I stretched thy joints to make thee even feet,
Yet still thou run'st more hobbling than is meet;
In better dress to trim thee was my mind,
But nought save homespun cloth i' th' house I find.
In this array 'mongst vulgars may'st thou roam.
In critic's hands beware thou dost not come,
And take thy way where yet thou art not known;
If for thy father asked, say thou hadst none;
And for thy mother, she alas is poor,
Which caused her thus to send thee out of door.

Here Conlon is moving from the first main section of her paper, which deals with Anne Bradstreet's earlier poems and the background against which she wrote them, to the second main section, which is concerned with a closer look at Bradstreet's later poetry. Conlon makes her transition effectively, using a quotation from Bradstreet's early work to introduce the point that there is "another voice" in the first volume of poems, "forceful, ironic, intelligent."

4

man 253). Any woman who attempted to join this company was apt to come to a bad end, as had the wife of
the governor of Hartford, Connecticut, who had suf-
fered insanity because, it was alleged, of her devo-
tion to reading and writing. There was also the example of the sister of Bradstreet's husband, disgraced
in her family for "Irregular Prophecying" and preach-
ing in England, as well as Bradstreet's friend Anne
Hutchinson, expelled by the Massachusetts Bay Colony
for listening to the inner voice of God rather than
to the elders of the Church (White 173-76).

Such consequences of speaking out may have
prompted Bradstreet's humility in her early verse,
which she describes meekly as the "ill-formed offspring of my feeble brain." She had hoped, she continues, to trim her "rambling brat" in better dress,
though "nought save homespun cloth i' th' house I
find" ("The Author to Her Book" 1, 9, 19). It is an
apt phrase to describe the mixture of pedantic learning, dull moralizing, and poetic cliché that made
the book popular in its own time. But another voice
also speaks out in this first volume, a forceful,
ironic, intelligent voice, as in these lines from
"In Honour of Queen Elizabeth":

Conlon's analyses of "Before the Birth of One of Her Children" and of "Contemplations" focus on the tension between the human and the spiritual in Bradstreet—the point asserted in the paper's thesis.

5

> Now say, have women worth? or have they
>
>   none?
>
> Or had they some, but with our Queen is't
>
>   gone?
>
> Nay masculines, you have thus taxed us
>
>   long,
>
> But she, though dead, will vindicate our
>
>   wrong.
>
> Let such as say our sex is void of reason,
>
> Know 'tis a slander now but once was
>
>   treason. (99-104)

As she set about revising her poems and adding to them
in the second edition, Anne Bradstreet drew upon this
voice. Instead of writing what she thought was expected of a Puritan poet, she now wrote what she felt,
drawing for material on the timeless events of a
woman's personal life. The tension generated by the
persistent conflict between the duty owed to God and
the human concerns of Bradstreet's everyday world
gives strength and vitality to these later poems.

A typical example is "Before the Birth of One
of Her Children," which expresses Bradstreet's
fears, well founded in the seventeenth century, of
dying in childbirth. Her sadness arises not from ter-
ror of the afterlife, for she had the Puritan's confi-

In each of these paragraphs, Conlon gives the title of the poem being quoted in the first sentence; citations to the poem later in the paragraph, therefore, need to provide only the appropriate line numbers.

6

dence in salvation, but from imagined grief at leaving her husband. The tears that dropped on her manuscript, she writes, fell also for her children, and
she begged her husband to "protect [them] from step-
dame's injury" (26).

   "Contemplations," by common agreement the most
successful of her poems, has as its underlying theme
the truth that earth as well as heaven declares the
glory of the Lord. Looking at the autumnal splendor
of the New England landscape, Bradstreet asks:

> If so much excellence abide below,
>
> How excellent is He that dwells on high,
>
> Whose power and beauty by his works we
>
> know? (10-12)

Though the poem unflinchingly faces the passing of
fragile beauty and human life into the everlasting-
ness of God, the poet nevertheless lingers for a long,
loving look by the river's bank with her senses full
and a "thousand fancies buzzing in my brain" (178).
"Contemplations" has been called the first American
nature poem (Waggoner 8).

   Another theme that evokes the best in Bradstreet
is the terrible mystery of the early death of children. Three of her grandchildren died within five

Again, ellipses and brackets indicate Conlon's changes in the original text of Bradstreet's poem:

But plants new set to be eradicate,
And buds new blown to have so short a date,
Is by His hand alone that guides nature and fate.

Conlon again returns explicitly to her thesis by pointing out Bradstreet's "submissiveness" and her "protest."

7

years, and Bradstreet's protest at this eradication
of "plants new set . . . [a]nd buds new blown" ("In
Memory of My Dear Grandchild Elizabeth Bradstreet"
17-18) is at first bitter, revealing a dark root of
anger and grief. In the end, as always, she submits:

> Such was His will, but why, let's not
>   dispute,
> With humble hearts and mouths put in the
>   dust,
> Let's say He's merciful as well as just.
> ("On My Dear Grandchild Simon Bradstreet"
> 10-12)

Along with the submissiveness, one hears in such
poems as this the persistent protest of Bradstreet's
heart against the desolate life in this new world.

One of the senseless accidents of life that the
Puritan was bound to accept as part of God's merciful
Providence was the loss of worldly goods. When the
Bradstreet house burned down through the careless-
ness of a servant, she lost not only her shelter from
the New England weather but all the little personal
possessions that had helped to make her new life tol-
erable. Compared to the modest wealth she had known
in England, her American treasures must have been

No colon is needed to introduce the quotation after the word *places,* because the quoted lines are grammatically part of the sentence that introduces them.

If a verse quotation begins in the middle of a line, indent the first line several additional spaces. Again, no introductory colon is needed here, because the quoted lines complete Conlon's own sentence.

In the paper's conclusion, Conlon deftly echoes her thesis by stressing the way in which the human concerns of Bradstreet's poetry represent a break from her Old-World Puritan roots.

8

paltry, but losing them was still painful, and her
grief was real as she looked at the places

> Where oft I sat and long did lie:
> Here stood that trunk, and there that
> chest,
> There lay that store I counted best.
> ("Some Verses upon the Burning of Our
> House" 28-30)

But Bradstreet well knew the Puritan's answer to such
tribulation. She might feel sorrow at the sight of
her treasures now in ashes, but

> when I could no longer look,
> I blest His name that gave and took,
> That laid my goods now in the dust. (17-19)

Bradstreet's later poems, in which the Old World
and its old history are forgotten and the New World
and its trees and small graves are remembered, assure
her a prominent place in the American tradition. The
recognition that came with the publication of her
first poems seems to have freed her to write poetry
about what she saw and touched and lost. These later
poems still stand, more than three hundred years after she wrote them, as honest testaments of the human
condition as one woman saw it.

1/2"

1"

9

Note

[1] Quotations from Bradstreet's works are taken from the Hensley edition. Line numbers are given for verse quotations.

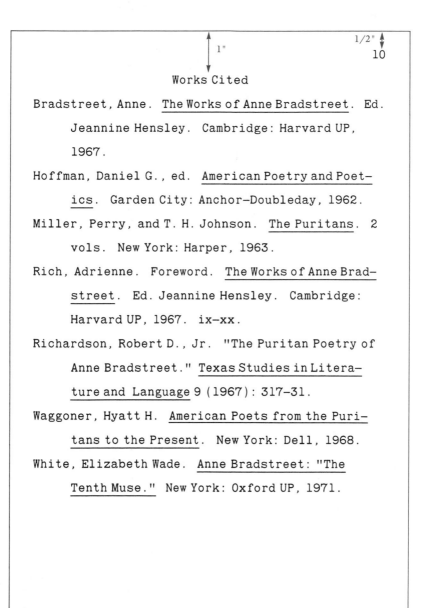

1"   1/2"
                10

Works Cited

Bradstreet, Anne. <u>The Works of Anne Bradstreet</u>. Ed.
  Jeannine Hensley. Cambridge: Harvard UP,
  1967.

Hoffman, Daniel G., ed. <u>American Poetry and Poet-
  ics</u>. Garden City: Anchor–Doubleday, 1962.

Miller, Perry, and T. H. Johnson. <u>The Puritans</u>. 2
  vols. New York: Harper, 1963.

Rich, Adrienne. Foreword. <u>The Works of Anne Brad-
  street</u>. Ed. Jeannine Hensley. Cambridge:
  Harvard UP, 1967. ix–xx.

Richardson, Robert D., Jr. "The Puritan Poetry of
  Anne Bradstreet." <u>Texas Studies in Literature and Language</u> 9 (1967): 317–31.

Waggoner, Hyatt H. <u>American Poets from the Puritans to the Present</u>. New York: Dell, 1968.

White, Elizabeth Wade. <u>Anne Bradstreet: "The
  Tenth Muse."</u> New York: Oxford UP, 1971.

Student Research Paper B: APA Documentation

Originally formulated more than sixty years ago to guide psychologists in the preparation of scholarly articles, the American Psychological Association's style of documentation is the norm today for professional publication not only in psychology but throughout the social sciences. This chapter will discuss and illustrate the features of APA documentation, explain the formatting of a paper prepared according to APA guidelines, and close with a sample student research paper documented in APA style.

6a Using APA documentation

APA documentation style resembles MLA documentation in its use of brief parenthetical references in the text to a list of full citations—called a reference list—at the end of the paper. But subtle differences distinguish the two methods of documentation. If you are already familiar with MLA documentation style, you will want to keep in mind the following distinctive characteristics of APA reference list citations.

1. Initials are always used in place of an author's first and middle names.
2. The author's name is always followed immediately by the date of his or her publication in parentheses. The remaining publication information comes later in the citation.
3. Not every major word in the title of a book or periodical article is capitalized; only the first word of the title, the first word of a subtitle, and any proper nouns in the title are capitalized.
4. The second and subsequent lines of each citation are indented three spaces, not five.
5. In general, APA documentation uses fewer abbreviations than MLA style; months of the year and names of universities, for example, are written out in full.

6b   APA reference list forms

Sections **6c** and **6d** will discuss the features of APA parenthetical citations and provide guidelines for formatting the components of a paper prepared in APA style. First, however, we need to examine some sample reference citations in APA format for the most frequently used types of source. (For additional information about APA citations, see the *Publication Manual of the American Psychological Association*, cited in item 3 below.)

Table of APA reference forms

Books

1. **Book by one author**
2. **Book by two or more authors**
3. **Book by a committee, commission, association, or other group**
4. **Anonymous book**
5. **Later or revised edition of a book**
6. **Edited book**

7. Translated book
8. Book in more than one volume
9. Republished book

Parts of books

10. Essay in a collection of essays by various authors
11. Journal or magazine article reprinted in a collection of essays by various authors

Articles in journals and magazines

12. Article in a journal paginated by the volume (continuous pagination)
13. Article in a journal paginated issue by issue
14. Article in a weekly magazine
15. Article in a monthly magazine

Articles in newspapers

16. Article in a newspaper
17. Letter to the editor

Other print sources

18. Book review
19. Dissertation, unpublished, microfilm copy
20. Dissertation, unpublished, manuscript copy
21. Encyclopedia article
22. Government document
23. Interview, published
24. Proceedings of a conference
25. Report

Nonprint sources

26. Computer software
27. Film, videotape, audiotape, slides, chart, artwork
28. Lecture, unpublished

Books

1. Book by one author

Hayes, J. R. (1978). Cognitive psychology: Think-

ing and creating. Homewood, IL: Dorsey Press.

- Capitalize only the first word of the title and the first word of the subtitle (and proper nouns in the title, if any).
- Add the U.S. Postal Service abbreviation for the state if the city of publication is not well known.
- For nonacademic publishers, use a shortened form of the company's name, omitting such terms as *Co., Inc.,* and *Publishers.* However, write out in full the names of university presses (see item 7 below).

2. Book by two or more authors

Clark, H. H., & Clark, E. V. (1977). Psychology and

language: An introduction to psycholinguistics.

New York: Harcourt.

Naylor, J. C., Pritchard, R. D., & Ilgen, D. R.

(1980). A theory of behavior in organizations.

New York: Academic Press.

- Regardless of the number of authors, give the names of all in inverted order, following each name with a comma and preceding the last name with an ampersand (&).

3. Book by a committee, commission, association, or other group

American Psychological Association. (1963). Pub-

lication manual of the American Psychological

Association (3rd ed.). Washington, DC: Author.

- When the author of the book is also its publisher, substitute the word *Author* for the name of the publisher at the end of the citation.
- The first parenthetical text citation to this work would begin with the joint author's name written out in full: (American Psychological Association [APA], 1963). Since the abbreviation of this association's name is a familiar one, subsequent parenthetical text citations may give only the abbreviation: (APA, 1963). See **6c**.

4. Anonymous book

Research in outdoor education: Summaries of doctoral studies. (1973). Washington, DC: American Association for Health, Physical Education, and Recreation.

- The parenthetical text citation for an anonymous work begins with the first two or three words of the title: (Research in Outdoor, 1973). See **6c**.

5. Later or revised edition of a book

Phelps, R. R. (1986). A guide to research in music education (3rd ed.). Metuchen, NJ: Scarecrow.

Jourard, S. M. (1971). The transparent self (rev. ed.). New York: Van Nostrand.

- When information in parentheses follows the title of a book, as it does here, no punctuation appears between the title and the parentheses.

6. Edited book

Halebsky, S. (Ed.). (1973). The sociology of the
  city. New York: Scribner's.
Stam, H. J., Rogers, T. B., & Gergen, K. J. (Eds.).
  (1987). The analysis of psychological theory:
  Metapsychological perspectives. Washington,
  DC: Hemisphere.

7. Translated book

Hauser, A. (1982). The sociology of art (K. J.
  Northcott, Trans.). Chicago: University of Chicago Press. (Original work published 1974)

- In parentheses after the title, supply the translator's name in normal order.
- End the citation with a parenthetical note giving the date of the book's original publication. Do not use punctuation within these parentheses.

8. Book in more than one volume

Ford, J. (1975). Paradigms and fairy tales: An
  introduction to the science of meanings (Vols.
  1-2). London: Routledge.

- After the title, indicate which volumes of the work you refer to in your paper; that information may differ from the total number of volumes in the work.

9. Republished book

```
Cottrell, F. (1970). Energy and society: The rela-
    tion between energy, social change, and economic
    development. Westport, CT: Greenwood Press.
    (Original work published 1955)
```

- The copyright page of this book indicates that it was originally issued in 1955 by a different publisher. Although information about the first publisher is not required in this citation, the original publication date is given in a parenthetical note at the end of the citation.

Parts of books

10. Essay in a collection of essays by various authors

```
Boskoff, A. (1964). Recent theories of social
    change. In W. J. Cahnman & A. Boskoff (Eds.),
    Sociology and history (pp. 140-157). New York:
    Free Press of Glencoe.
Tawney, J. W. (1977). Educating severely handi-
    capped children and their parents through tele-
    communications. In N. G. Haring & L. J. Brown
    (Eds.), Teaching the severely handicapped
    (Vol. 2, pp. 315-340). New York: Grune & Stratton.
```

- Follow the title of the essay by the name(s) of the editor(s) of the book in which it is contained, the title of the book, and the pages on which the essay is found.
- For an essay in a multivolume collection, include the appropriate volume number as shown in the second example.

- Note that when inclusive page numbers are provided in an APA citation, the complete second number is used (not 315–40, but 315–*340*).

11. **Journal or magazine article reprinted in a collection of essays by various authors**

    Motokawa, K. (1965). Retinal traces and visual

    perception of movement. In I. M. Spigel (Ed.),

    Readings in the study of visually perceived

    movement (pp. 288–303). New York: Harper.

    (Reprinted from the Journal of Experimental

    Psychology, 1953, 45, 369–377)

- When information about an article's earlier publication is noted in the collection you are using, provide it in parentheses at the end of the citation.

Articles in journals and magazines

12. **Article in a journal paginated by the volume (continuous pagination)**

    Webster, G. R. (1989). Partisanship in American

    presidential, senatorial, and gubernatorial

    elections in ten western states. Political

    Geography Quarterly, 8, 161–179.

- Most periodicals published quarterly or less frequently use continuous pagination for all the issues published in a single year; that is, if the year's first issue ends with page 125, the second issue begins with page 126. The citation to such a

periodical includes the name of the journal (underlined), the volume number (separately underlined), and the first and last pages of the article (without the abbreviation *pp.*).
- Do not enclose the title of the article in quotation marks.

13. Article in a journal paginated issue by issue

Maranto, C. D. (1987). Continuing concerns in music

therapy ethics. Music Therapy, 6(2), 59–63.

- When each issue of a journal begins with page 1, include the issue number (2) in parentheses immediately after the underlined volume number (6).

14. Article in a weekly magazine

Jaroff, L. (1989, July 3). Fury on the sun. Time,

pp. 46–55.

Running up a global tab. (1989, July 10). Time,

p. 47.

- Give the date with the year first, followed by the month, unabbreviated, and the day.
- End the citation with the page number or numbers of the article, preceded by *p.* ("page") or *pp.* ("pages").
- For an anonymous article, begin the citation with the title.

15. Article in a monthly magazine

Hill, J. V. (1989, May). The design and procurement

of training simulators. Educational Technology,

pp. 26–27.

Healthy eating in Europe. (1989, May). World

Health, p. 30.

Articles in newspapers

16. Article in a newspaper

Freitag, M. (1989, August 17). The battle over

medical costs. New York Times, pp. 25, 28.

U.S. panel weighs birth pill warning. (1989, March

29). Chicago Sun-Times, p. 2.

- If an article is continued on nonconsecutive pages, give all page numbers, separated by commas: pp. 25, 28.

17. Letter to the editor

Capezza, D. (1989, July 13). Of course, oil spills

can be prevented [Letter to the editor]. New York

Times, p. A22.

- Follow the editor's title (if one exists) by a bracketed notation identifying the piece as a letter.

Other print sources

18. Book review

Kimble, G. A. (1988). Psychology's brief history

[Review of Historical foundations of mod-

ern psychology]. Contemporary Psychology,

33, 878-879.

Belotti, M. (1988). [Review of The paradox of pov-

erty: A reappraisal of economic development policy].

Journal of Economic Literature, 26, 1233-1234.

- If the review has a title, give it before the bracketed notation identifying the piece as a review.
- Note that the name of the author of the work being reviewed does not appear in the citation.

19. Dissertation, unpublished, microfilm copy

```
Johnson, T. P. (1989). The social environment and
    health. Dissertation Abstracts International,
    49, 3514A. (University Microfilms No. 8903561)
```

- Use this format if your source is a university microfilm copy of a dissertation. Note that the date given refers to this volume of *Dissertation Abstracts International,* not the date of the dissertation itself.

20. Dissertation, unpublished, manuscript copy

```
Johnson, T. P. (1989). The social environment and
    health (Doctoral dissertation, University of
    Kentucky, 1988). Dissertation Abstracts In-
    ternational, 49, 3514A.
```

- Use this format if your source is a manuscript copy of a dissertation. When the dates of the dissertation and of the publication of its abstract in *Dissertation Abstracts International* differ, as they do here, the parenthetical text citation includes both: (Johnson, 1988/1989).

21. Encyclopedia article

```
Dashiell, J. F. (1983). Behaviorism. In Ency-
    clopedia Americana (Vol. 3, pp. 469–471).
    Danbury, CT: Grolier.
```

- Treat an encyclopedia article the same as an article in a multi-volume collection of essays by different authors (see item 10 above).

22. Government document

U.S. Women's Bureau. (1975). Handbook on women

  workers. Washington, DC: U.S. Government Print-

  ing Office.

23. Interview, published

Lyman, F. (1988, January). [Interview with Maggie

  Kuhn, founder of the Gray Panthers]. The Pro-

  gressive, pp. 29–31.

- If an interview has a title, insert the title before the bracketed notation that identifies the piece and its subject (see item 17 above).

24. Proceedings of a conference

Genaway, D. C. (Ed.). (1983). Conference on inte-

  grated online library systems. Canfield, OH:

  Genaway & Associates.

Stilson, D. W. (1957). A multidimensional psycho-

  physical method for investigating visual form.

  In J. W. Wulfeck & J. H. Taylor (Eds.), Proceed-

  ings of a Symposium Sponsored by the Armed

  Forces–NRC Committee on Vision (pp. 54–64).

  Washington, DC: National Academy of Sciences–

  National Research Council.

- Use the first form for a citation to the collected proceedings of a conference, the second for a citation to a single article in such a collection.

25. Report

Butler, E. W., Chapin, F. S., Hemmens, G. C., Kaiser, E. J., Stegman, M. A., & Weiss, S. F. (1969). Moving behavior and residential choice: A national survey (National Cooperative Highway Research Program Rep. No. 81). Chapel Hill: University of North Carolina, Center for Urban and Regional Studies.

Price, M. E., & Botein, M. (1973). Cable television: Citizen participation after the franchise (Re search Rep. No. R–1139–NSF). Santa Monica, CA: Rand.

- If the report has been given a number, supply it in parentheses after the title.

Nonprint sources

26. Computer software

Etter T., & Chamberlain, W. (1984). Racter [Computer program]. Northbrook, IL: Mindscape.

27. Film, videotape, audiotape, slides, charts, artwork

Messecar, R. (Author & Producer/Editor), & Hales, D. (Author). (1982). Theater of the night:

The science of sleep and dreams [Film]. Pleas-

antville, NY: Human Relations Media.

Jordan, P. (Producer & Director). (1974). Preju-

dice: Causes, consequences, cures [Videotape].

Carlsbad, CA: CRM Films.

- Identify the functions of major contributors in parentheses after their names.
- Identify the medium in brackets after the title of the work.

28. Lecture, unpublished

Zappen, J. P. (1989, March). Scientific rhetoric

in the nineteenth and early twentieth centuries.

Paper presented at the Conference on College Com-

position and Communication, Seattle, WA.

- Include the month of the meeting or conference at which the lecture was delivered.

6c   Citing sources in APA style

APA text citations, like MLA citations, are inserted into the text parenthetically. But APA parenthetical citations differ from MLA citations in three ways:

1. The APA citation includes the author's name and the year of publication of the source. The page number is added only when a quotation is being cited.
2. The elements in an APA parenthetical citation are separated by commas.
3. The abbreviations *p.* and *pp.* are used with page numbers.

Compare the following examples of parenthetical citations in APA style with the corresponding MLA citations described in **4c**.

1. Quotations

As in MLA format, the parenthetical citation in the text comes *after* the quotation marks that close the quotation but *before* the sentence's end punctuation:

Parenthetical citation in text

The definitive biography of Mahatma Gandhi remains
to be written. As one Gandhi scholar has explained,
"Multivolume works written by Gandhi's former colleagues and published in India are comprehensive in
scope, but their objectivity suffers from the authors' reverent regard for their subject" (Juergensmeyer, 1984, p. 294).

Citation in reference list

Juergensmeyer, M. (1984). The Gandhi revival--A
review article. Journal of Asian Studies, 43,
293-298.

Below are some variations on this basic method of documenting quotations.

Setting off a long quotation

A quotation of more than forty words is set off from the text and indented five spaces from the left margin. Such a quotation is commonly introduced with a colon, and the parenthetical citation is placed after the end punctuation:

Parenthetical citation in text

One editor suggests that photographers trying to publish their work should aim to surpass--not just
equal--the photographs they see in print:

```
Editors know where they can get pictures like
the ones they've already published. If you want
to get noticed, you have to take pictures better
than those.  This is especially true if you are
looking for assignments rather than to sell ex-
isting pictures.  Why take a chance on a new pho-
tographer who will come up with no better than
what you already have, an editor might reason?
(Scully, 1984, p. 33)
```

Citation in reference list
```
Scully, J.  (1984, May).  Seeing pictures.  Modern
    Photography, pp. 28-33.
```

Incorporating the author's name into the text

If you introduce a quotation by mentioning the author's name in your text, use only the author's last name, unless first initials are needed to distinguish between two authors with the same surname. Follow the author's name immediately with the year of the source's publication in parentheses. The page number, also in parentheses, comes after the quotation:

Parenthetical citation in text
```
The English, notes Altick (1969), are obsessed by
love for their dogs:  "Walking dogs is a ritual that
proceeds independently of weather, cataclysms, and
the movements of the planets; they are led or carried
everywhere, into department stores, fishmongers',
greengrocers', buses, trains" (p. 286).
```

Citation in reference list

```
Altick, R. D. (1969). To be in England. New York:
    Norton.
```

Citing a work by more than one author

If your source was written by two authors, include the names of both in the parenthetical text citation, following the same order in which the names are printed in the original source:

Parenthetical citation in text

```
Selvin and Wilson (1984) argue that "a concern for
effective writing is not a trivial elevation of form
over content. Good writing is a condition, slowly
achieved, of . . . being what one means to be" (p.
207).
```

or

```
Two sociologists argue that "a concern for effective
writing is not a trivial elevation of form over con-
tent. Good writing is a condition, slowly achieved,
of . . . being what one means to be" (Selvin & Wilson,
1984, p. 207).
```

Citation in reference list

```
Selvin, H. C., & Wilson, E. K. (1984). On sharpening
    sociologists' prose. Sociological Quarterly,
    25, 205-222.
```

Note the following variations on this rule when more than two authors are involved:

1. When the source was written by three to five authors, give all their names in the first parenthetical text citation, but in subsequent citations include in the parenthetical text citation the name of the first author only, followed by the abbreviation *et al.* (Latin for "and others"; the abbreviation is not underlined): (O'Malley et al., 1990, p. 101).
2. When six or more authors are involved, give the name of the first author only, followed by the abbreviation *et al.*, in all parenthetical text citations.

Note, however, that the reference list citation includes the names of all authors, regardless of the number.

Citing an anonymous work

If you quote an anonymous work, use the first two or three words of the title in your parenthetical text citation. Place the titles of articles in quotation marks (but note that they are not enclosed in quotation marks in the reference list citation), and underline the titles of books. Capitalize all major words of the title in the parenthetical text citation (but not in the reference list citation).

Parenthetical citation in text

Environmentalists protested that a recent study of

the plan to spray herbicides on marijuana "systemati-

cally underestimated the possibility of damage from

such spraying and exaggerated the benefits to be

achieved by a spraying program" ("Marijuana Spray-

ing," 1984, p. 14).

Citation in reference list

Marijuana spraying opposed. (1984, August 22). New

York Times, p. 14.

Citing a multivolume work

The volume number of a multivolume work appears in the parenthetical text citation only when the reference list citation indicates that more than one volume of the work has been consulted (see item 8 in **6b** above).

Parenthetical citation in text

The medieval manor house dominated nearby cottages "not only because it was better built, but above all because it was almost invariably designed for defence" (Bloch, 1961, Vol. 2, p. 300).

Citation in reference list

Bloch, M. (1961). Feudal society (L. A. Manyon, Trans., Vols. 1-2). Chicago: University of Chicago Press. (Original work published 1939)

Citing two works by the same author

If the sources you use include more than one work by the same author, the date that you give in each parenthetical text citation may alone be sufficient to indicate which work is being cited. If more than one work by an author has been published in the same year, however, differentiate among works by adding lowercase letters to the dates in *both* the reference list and the parenthetical text citations:

Parenthetical citations in text

(Gilbert, 1985a, p. 112)

(Gilbert, 1985b, pp. 164-165)

Citations in reference list

```
Gilbert, L. A. (1985a). Dimensions of same-gender
    student-faculty role-model relationships. Sex
    Roles, 12, 111-123.
Gilbert, L. A. (1985b). Measures of psychological
    masculinity and femininity: A comment on Gaddy,
    Glass, and Arnkoff. Journal of Counseling Psy-
    chology, 32, 163-166.
```

2. Paraphrases

As noted above, APA documentation style departs from MLA style significantly in the case of paraphrasing. In APA style the parenthetical text citation does not include a page number when the writer is paraphrasing, rather than quoting, a source.

Parenthetical citation in text (author's name in parenthetical citation)

```
The steadily growing role of television in politics
has helped to shift attention away from the politi-
cians' stands on issues to the way they appear before
the camera (Meyrowitz, 1984).
```

Citation in reference list

```
Meyrowitz, J. (1984, July). Politics in the video
    eye: Where have all the heroes gone? Psychology
    Today, pp. 46-51.
```

Parenthetical citation in text (author's name incorporated into text)

One effect of the microscope's development in the late 1600s, Fussell (1965) points out, was to change attitudes toward insects. Whereas people in the seventeenth century had considered insects innocuous creatures, eighteenth-century men and women, exposed for the first time to drawings of magnified insect bodies, regarded them as hideous and contemptible.

Citation in reference list

Fussell, P. (1965). The rhetorical world of Augustan humanism: Ethics and imagery from Swift to Burke. London: Oxford University Press.

<u>6d</u> Formatting a paper in APA style

The manuscript style described by the American Psychological Association in its *Publication Manual* is intended primarily for authors who are submitting articles for consideration by professional journals. The writers of the manual note, therefore, that its requirements may need to be modified for use in undergraduate classes.

In the guidelines below, only the APA's title-page requirements have been modified, in order to allow for inclusion of the course number, the name of the instructor, and the date on which the paper is submitted. Check with your instructor for supplementary or alternative instructions.

1. Paper

Using a typewriter or computer printer with a fresh ribbon, type or print out your research paper on standard 8½-by-11-inch white bond. Avoid dot-matrix computer printers unless they print clearly and legibly. Do not use onionskin or erasable paper.

2. Spacing and margins

Double-space everything in your paper—text, long quotations, footnotes, and reference list. Double-space as well between page headings (such as "References") and the first line of text on the page.

Leave a 1½-inch margin on the top, bottom, and sides of each page. In the upper right corner of each page (including the first), about three-quarters of an inch from the top of the page, type a short title, consisting of the first two or three words of the paper's title. The short title guards against pages becoming separated and misplaced. Double-space after the short title, and number the pages consecutively with Arabic numbers typed under its last character; do not use abbreviations such as *p.* with page numbers. Double-space again on each page to introduce a page heading or continue the text. Type a maximum of twenty-five lines of text on each page.

3. Title page

On four double-spaced lines centered on the title page, provide the following information:

1. The title of your paper, not enclosed in quotation marks or underlined. Capitalize only the first letters of important words in the title. Double-space between the lines of a title typed on more than one line.
2. Your name.
3. The course for which the paper is being submitted, followed by a comma and your professor's name: Psychology 100, Professor Sharon March.
4. The date of submission.

Don't forget to include your short title and first page number on double-spaced lines in the upper right corner. See the sample title page on page 136.

4. Abstract page

In APA style, a paper begins with an abstract, or summary, of its contents, typed on a separate page. The abstract should be about one hundred words long; it should present the purpose or thesis of your paper, indicate the types of sources you investigated, and state the conclusions you arrived at.

Double-space after typing the page number, and center the word *Abstract* on the next line. Double-space again, and type your abstract in block style—that is, without the usual paragraph indentions. See the sample abstract on page 137.

5. Text pages

The text of your paper begins on page 3. Double-space after typing the short title and page number, and center your title on the page. Double-space again, and begin the first line of the paper.

6. References page

In APA format, the sources used in a research paper are listed alphabetically on a final page, with the heading "References" centered at the top of the page. Do not underline this heading or enclose it in quotation marks. Double-space after this heading and give the citation for the first source used; double-space between lines of each citation and between citations. Alphabetize an anonymous source by the first significant word in the reference list citation. See the sample reference list on pages 157–158.

7. Footnotes page

As in MLA format, content notes, if any, are given on a separate page. In APA format, this page *follows* the reference list page or pages. At the top of the page, center the heading "Footnotes" (or "Footnote," if only one note is given); again, do not underline this heading or enclose it in quotation marks. Double-space between this heading and the first footnote. Begin each footnote with a superior number indented five spaces; do not leave a space between the superior number and the first word of each footnote. Double-space between and within footnotes. See the sample footnotes page on page 159.

6e   Sample student paper

Cyndi Lopardo's "Career versus Motherhood: The Debate over Education for Women at the Turn of the Century" is a good example of a paper based on what are called primary sources. Primary sources are raw data, documents, or evidence—for example, the results of experiments; original letters and diaries; historical records; and eyewitness accounts of events. Secondary sources, in contrast, are other writers' commentaries on or analyses of primary works. In this paper Cyndi's primary sources are published articles from the 1890s, from which she has acquired a firsthand sense of contemporary ideas about the education of women.

Cyndi's task in the paper is the same one that confronts every researcher whose work is based on primary sources—to analyze the data, draw conclusions about it, and then present and defend those conclusions to her readers. Of course, the final paper does not include every article Cyndi examined. Instead, having used her reading to develop a thesis, Cyndi selects the articles that provide the best evidence for the point she wants to make: that while increasing numbers of women had access to higher education by the end of the nineteenth century, there was widespread feeling that colleges should be specifically training women for motherhood rather than for possible professional careers outside the home.

One of the strengths of this paper is Cyndi's handling of her evidence. In the first place, she blends quotation, paraphrase, and summary well, providing just the right amount of detail necessary for the reader to understand each article she cites. Throughout the paper, moreover, she clearly introduces each piece of evidence, indicating the specific point it is intended to illustrate. Cyndi also effectively groups together similar pieces of evidence and points out their similarities to her readers. The result of all these strategies is a well-organized paper that convincingly supports its thesis.

Career versus Motherhood

1

Career versus Motherhood: The Debate over Education

for Women at the Turn of the Century

Cyndi Lopardo

Education 100, Professor Karen J. Blair

March 20, 1990

Abstract

By 1890, the opening of colleges for women and the advent of coeducation had settled the issue of women's access to higher education. But another question remained unresolved: the purpose of a college education in a woman's life. Articles published during the 1890s on the goals of higher education for women suggest that, despite the professional accomplishments of many educated women in the nineteenth century, social forces were at work to keep women's education focused on the enrichment of home and family. A woman's right to a professional career outside the home would not be recognized until the next century.

Lopardo's opening paragraphs effectively provide background and focus for the paper. The first paragraph identifies educational opportunity as a key element in the women's movement of the nineteenth century; the second focuses on the status of higher education for women in the 1890s; and the third isolates a specific issue in discussions about women's education during that decade. Note the effective transitions between these paragraphs: the first sentence of each paragraph smoothly refers to the key idea in the preceding one.

The original text of the passage that Lopardo quotes from the Seneca Falls Declaration is as follows:

> He has denied her the facilities for obtaining a thorough education, all colleges being closed against her.

APA style permits changing the first letter of a quotation from uppercase to lowercase (or vice versa) without brackets. (In MLA style, such a change would have to be indicated: "[h]e has denied. . . .") Lopardo clarifies the quotation by using brackets to substitute *woman* for *her*.

1 1/2"

Career versus Motherhood: The Debate over Education
for Women at the Turn of the Century
The origins of the modern women's movement have
frequently been traced to the convention of women
organized by Elizabeth Cady Stanton and Lucretia Mott
in Seneca Falls, New York, on July 19 and 20, 1848.
Besides launching the drive for women's suffrage,
the Seneca Falls Convention produced a major document
in the history of women's rights. The Declaration
of Sentiments and Resolutions, modeled after the Declaration of Independence, listed both the grievances
and the aspirations of politically active women in
the nineteenth century. To this document the begin-
nings of educational opportunities for women can also
be traced, for one of its stated grievances against
man was that "he has denied [woman] the facilities
for obtaining a thorough education, all colleges being closed against her" ("Seneca Falls Declaration,"
1973, p. 316).

The participants in the Seneca Falls Convention
could not have foreseen how quickly that inequity
would be remedied. By 1890, many of the women's colleges that are today associated with excellence in

In APA style, paraphrased material is cited by author and date alone. Page numbers are included only after quotations.

Lopardo's third paragraph introduces the evidence she will present—published articles from the 1890s—and ends with the thesis she will argue.

APA style encourages the use of subheadings to highlight a paper's organization. Double-space before and after a subheading; do not underline or capitalize it. In a more technical paper (for example, one reporting the results of an experiment), the problem being investigated would be introduced in the opening paragraphs and the rest of the paper would be divided with the following headings: Method, Results, Discussion.

Career versus Motherhood

4

education had opened their doors——among them Mt.
Holyoke, Vassar, Smith, Wellesley, Radcliffe,
Bryn Mawr, and Barnard. Even more significant, by
this time nearly two-thirds of all the nation's
colleges and universities were coeducational
(Buckler, 1897).

On the surface, then, the story of women's education in the nineteenth century would seem to be one
of rapidly expanding opportunities. By the end of
the century, however, a new debate was raging——not
over women's access to higher education, but over
the purpose of such an education in a woman's life.
An examination of articles written during the 1890s
on the goals of higher education for women leads one
to conclude that equality of opportunity was not yet
within women's grasp. Higher education did not open
up new spheres of activity for most women at the end
of the nineteenth century; instead, these articles
suggest that powerful social forces were at work to
keep education for women focused on the enrichment
and enhancement of home and family.

Supporters of Opportunities for Women

To be sure, some educators of the time did call

Quotations of more than forty words are set off by indenting five spaces from the left margin. Ellipsis marks indicate omitted material.

Career versus Motherhood

5

for broader educational and professional opportunities for women. Butler (1896), for example, criti-
cized the ways in which women's development was re-
tarded by prevailing attitudes in society—for example, by the belief that girls' elementary and secondary education should not be as rigorous as boys'.
Franklin (1898) agreed that what we today would call
social conditioning was responsible for the gap between the accomplishments of men and those of women.
The "youthful dreams and aspirations of a gifted boy
cluster around high achievement and resounding
fame," he explained, "because all that he hears and
reads tends to arouse in him such ambitions" (p. 46).
In contrast, the girl is taught to focus her life
on "the conquest of men by beauty and charm" (pp. 46-
47). No wonder, therefore, that women's professional accomplishments had not equaled those of men:

> Men who have had the spark of genius or even of
> talent in them have been spurred to effort by
> all their surroundings, by the traditions of
> the race, by rivalry with their comrades, by
> the admiration which the opposite sex accords
> to brilliant achievements. . . . What of all

The superior number *1* refers to a content note, which is found at the end of the paper on the page following the reference list.

Note how the opening sentences of this paragraph organize the material that follows. The first sentence is transitional, contrasting the critics to be presented here with the supporters of opportunities for women discussed above. The second sentence identifies one group of critics, those who attempted to belittle women's professional accomplishments. Since Buckler is then introduced as a member of this group, the reader is prepared for a discussion that illustrates her treatment of women's accomplishments in this way.

Career versus Motherhood

6

this has there been for women? How many have
been so placed as to even think of an intellectual career as a possibility? . . . The very ab-
sorption in a high intellectual interest . . .
was, in the case of girls, up to the last two
or three decades, universally condemned and
repressed and thwarted even in the most cultivated families. (p. 43)[1]

Two Groups of Critics

Such defenses of women's intellectual rights
were, however, far less typical of the 1890s than
criticism of wider educational and professional opportunities for women was. The critics could hardly
ignore women's recent achievements in such previ-
ously male fields as science, law, and medicine, but
one group of these critics found ways of denigrating
those accomplishments in order to assert the need
for a college curriculum for women that was focused
on the home and family. Buckler (1897) is representa-
tive of this group. On the one hand, she concedes
that "there is no walk of life which, in some quarter
of the globe at least, is not open to [women]" (p.
302). But on the other hand, even as she enumerates

In the quotation from Buckler, Lopardo underlines the phrase *the good of the community* to emphasize the standard by which Buckler is judging women's accomplishments. Following APA style, she inserts the phrase *italics added* in brackets immediately after the underlined phrase to indicate that she has added underscoring (emphasis) not found in the original text.

Career versus Motherhood

7

women's accomplishments in professional life, Buckler concludes that women have never "achieved anything absolutely first-rate, whether as creation or
as discovery" (p. 303), and that there is little
chance they ever will:

> If women were ever intellectually equal to men,
> when and why did they begin to fall behind? And
> if they never were equal, how can they hope to
> catch up now, when masculine education is ad-
> vancing at as great a rate as feminine? (p. 308)

Why should women pursue a professional career if they
are thus doomed to second-rate accomplishments? Or,
as Buckler phrases the question, "Is it for the good
of the community [italics added] that she should en-
gage in these higher branches [of literature, science, and art]?" (p. 296). In Buckler's view, wom-
en's professional accomplishments have been so
meager as to be inconsequential to the community at
large. Instead, she asserts, women should find satisfaction "in assisting and carrying out the cre-
ations of men. For it is in this subordinate relation
that women can probably find their truest and widest
sphere, that of Influence" (pp. 308-309).

An effective transitional sentence indicates that Bolton is also included in the first group of critics, those who sought to diminish women's professional accomplishments.

Lopardo now moves to a second group of critics, those who felt that the college curriculum for women should place greater emphasis on domestic issues. Note the transitions within this paragraph that link its main examples: Brown (1896), *for example,* agrees. . . . Backus (1899) *also* praises. . . .

Career versus Motherhood

8

Bolton (1898) approaches the issue of college education for women in a similar way. She begins by cataloging women's accomplishments from biblical times to the present, but in spite of this evidence she concludes, paradoxically, that "[women's] genius has but a limited field; while many have obtained fame through their knowledge of mathematics and its applications to astronomy, they show but little aptitude for the natural sciences, and rarely exhibit any inventive faculty" (pp. 510-511). A life of learning, she claims, can therefore never offer a woman the same fulfillment as being "a happy wife and good mother" (p. 511). Echoing Buckler (1897), Bolton suggests that if women's education is to be put to a worthwhile purpose, it should be to "assist some loved one to perfect his researches" (p. 511).

A second group of critics took pains to praise the new educational opportunities open to women, but warned of the dangers of a college curriculum for women that neglected domestic issues. Brown (1896), for example, agrees with Franklin and Butler that "every human being, man or woman, should have all the education that he can take" (p. 431). But she defends

When citing two works by the same author, include the dates of both works in parentheses, separated by a comma: (Smith, 1895, 1898) or Smith (1895, 1898). If you use a parenthetical citation to cite two or more works by different authors, arrange them in alphabetical order and separate them with a semicolon: (Jones, 1988; Smith, 1990).

women's education only in terms of its usefulness
as preparation for motherhood, and she concludes by
warning that "whatever in the education of girls
draws them away from [the home] is an injury to civili-
zation" (p. 432). Backus (1899) also praises the "new
womanhood" of her decade, citing "mental ambition"
as the "dominating force among intelligent modern
women" (p. 461). But she leaves little room for such
amibition in her conception of women's higher education. Instead, her defense of the current college
curriculum for women rests solely on its contribution
to motherhood:

> Can we not secure better returns from college
> training [of women] if the needs of the family,
> the ideals of wifehood, be kept steadily in the
> view of our daughters—the home be made the cri-
> terion for all mental effort exercised without
> the home? (p. 461)

Increasing Conservatism

At least some critics of higher education for
women during the 1890s became more conservative as
the twentieth century approached. Two articles by
Smith (1895, 1898), for example, illustrate the ap-

The date in parentheses after the second mention of *Smith* indicates which of her articles is being discussed in this paragraph.

As above, Lopardo uses brackets to insert words that make the quoted passage clearer. The original version begins as follows:

> In fact, nobody knew very well what she was there for; it seemed only fair that she should "have a chance too," but a chance for what? . . .

Career versus Motherhood

10

parently increasing pressure for domestic education
at the college level. Like Brown (1896) and Backus
(1899), Smith (1895) applauds the new educational
opportunities open to women whose "distinctive intellectual bent demanded some other outlet than
housekeeping for their energies. They wished to
teach in the higher schools, or to enter the professions of literature, law, or medicine" (p. 27). As
Smith surveys the recent history of higher education for women, however, it becomes clear that her
own vision of women's education is a significantly
narrower one:

> In fact, nobody knew very well what [a woman]
> was [in college] for; it seemed only fair that
> she should "have a chance too," but a chance for
> what? Why, to marry, of course! But nobody
> ever said that aloud, and nobody thought of
> adapting her training to her probable and desir-
> able business in life. (p. 28)

In the future, Smith says hopefully, the "tendency
to emphasize the profession of wifehood and motherhood in its proper relations will be increasingly
controlling in all education of women" (p. 33).

Lopardo effectively summarizes Smith's entire article of 1898 in a single paragraph. Note the key passages from the last paragraph of the article that she has selected to quote (the quoted passages are italicized):

> If to all these practical and utilitarian attainments the mother can add *the graces of culture in music or art or literature,* she may give the child a background for education and a resource in life beyond the power of statistics to estimate. The elevation, enrichment, and sweetening of the family life by these contributions from the mother's own storehouse of culture are a safeguard against temptation from without not to be matched by legislation or training, or even by church influence. To *make the household sweet, wholesome, dignified,* a place of growth, is certainly a profession requiring not merely the best training, but a specific training adapted to those ends.

Lopardo's concluding paragraph returns smoothly to the note on which the paper began—the Seneca Falls Convention of 1848. Here she introduces a second quotation from the Seneca Falls Declaration—a passage demanding equality in career opportunities—to underscore her concluding point, that although women had access to higher education by the end of the century, they had still not gained the right to use that education in a professional career outside the home.

Career versus Motherhood

11

At the end of the decade, Smith (1898) returns to this topic, but in an even more reactionary way. Now she calls the idea of having women pursue the same college curriculum as men an "experiment" (p. 522) that has failed. In its place, she proposes in detail a curriculum that will enable a woman to "make the household sweet, wholesome, dignified" (p. 525)—that is, a course of study emphasizing manual training, hygiene, "standards of honor and honesty," and "the graces of culture in music or art or literature" (p. 524).

Conclusions

Clearly the statistics regarding higher education for women at the end of the nineteenth century do not tell the whole story. It is true that the question of women's access to higher education had been resolved in the half-century since the Seneca Falls Convention, for most of the nation's colleges and universities had opened their doors to women. But another Seneca Falls resolution—one calling for "equal participation with men in the various trades, professions, and commerce" ("Seneca Falls Declaration," 1973, p. 317)—was far from fulfilled. Al-

Career versus Motherhood

12

though the education of women had become socially
acceptable, it remained focused on the enrichment
of home and family life; the intellectual life available to women could be pursued only as a sort of hobby.
The battle for the right to an education that was truly
equivalent to men's and for the right to a career outside the home remained to be fought in the next century.

Career versus motherhood

13

References

Backus, H. H. (1899, February 25). Should the
college train for motherhood? Outlook, pp. 461-
463.

Bolton, H. I. (1898, August). Women in science.
Popular Science Monthly, pp. 505-511.

Brown, H. D. (1896, March 7). How shall we educate
our girls? Outlook, pp. 431-432.

Buckler, G. G. (1897). The lesser man. North American Review, 165, 296-309.

Butler, N. M. (1896, April 4). The right training
of girls under sixteen. Outlook, pp. 626-627.

Franklin, F. (1898). The intellectual powers of
woman. North American Review, 166, 40-53.

The Seneca Falls declaration of sentiments and
resolutions. (1973). In H. S. Commager (Ed.),
Documents of American History (Vol. 1., pp. 315-
317). Englewood Cliffs: Prentice.

Smith, M. R. (1895, November). Recent tendencies
in the education of women. Popular Science
Monthly, pp. 27-33.

Smith, M. R. (1898, August). Education for domestic
life. Popular Science Monthly, pp. 521-525.

Career versus motherhood

14

Woodworth, R. S. (1933). Ladd–Franklin, Christine. In D. Malone (Ed.), Dictionary of American Biography (Vol. 10, pp. 528–530). New York: Scribner's.

Footnote

[1]Franklin's liberal perspective on the issue of professional careers for women can perhaps be explained by a biographical detail: he was married to the well-known psychologist Christine Ladd-Franklin. Although Ladd-Franklin fulfilled the doctoral requirements at Johns Hopkins University in 1882 and went on to a distinguished career in teaching and research at Columbia University, Johns Hopkins refused to award her a degree until 1926 because it did not officially recognize women as graduate students (Woodworth, 1933).

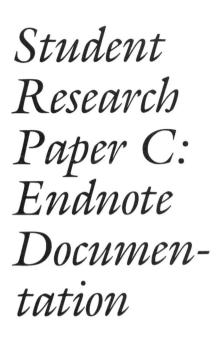

Student Research Paper C: Endnote Documentation

T hough abandoned by the Modern Language Association in 1984 in favor of the documentation style examined in Chapters **3** and **4**, endnote documentation remains in wide use in other humanities fields. This method of documentation inserts superior numbers (numbers raised a half-line) into the text to refer to citations that are then collected together on pages at the end of the paper. (A more complicated alternative not considered here is to place the appropriate notes at the bottom of each page; in that case they are called footnotes.)

This chapter discusses the key features of endnotes, provides a list of note forms for various kinds of citations, and offers a sample student research paper documented with endnotes.

7a   Using endnotes

Anyone who is familiar with the current style of MLA documentation will find the transition to using endnotes an easy one.

1. Features of endnotes

In place of the parenthetical citation in the text prescribed in MLA documentation, the writer using endnotes inserts a slightly raised number in the text corresponding to a citation given on note pages that follow the paper. The raised numbers inserted in the text do not start over with *1* on each page but run consecutively throughout the paper. Content notes, if any, do not appear on a separate note page but are intermingled with citations to sources.

Endnote forms differ from MLA Works Cited forms in five major ways.

1. The first line of an endnote is indented five spaces; subsequent lines are not indented (the reverse of Works Cited citations).
2. Authors' names are always presented in normal rather than inverted order.
3. Publication information for books is enclosed in parentheses.
4. In general, where MLA Works Cited forms separate elements with periods, endnote forms connect them with commas. However, no punctuation ever comes before parentheses unless the word before the parentheses is an abbreviation that ends in a period.
5. An endnote always ends with a page citation, unless (1) the note refers to the entire work being cited, or (2) the source is one without pages (for example, computer software, a film, an interview, or a lecture).

2. Features of the endnote page

In the center of the endnote page, one inch from the top, type the word *Notes,* not underlined or in quotation marks. Double-space, indent five spaces, and type a slightly raised *1*. Leave a space after the raised number before beginning the note; do not indent the second and subsequent lines of the note. Continue in the same manner with the rest of the paper's notes, double-spacing within and between notes. A bibliography page following the page or pages of endnotes is optional; if included, it is arranged like an MLA Works Cited page but given the heading "Bibliography."

In citations to a source for which full publication information has been given in an earlier note, provide only the author's last name (or a shortened form of the title, if it is an anonymous work) and the page number:

First citation

¹ Alice Walker, <u>The Color Purple</u> (New York: Harcourt, 1982) 44.

Subsequent citation

² Walker 70-71.

If the endnotes include citations to two works by the same author, subsequent citations include a shortened form of the appropriate title to distinguish between them.

First citations

¹ Alice Walker, <u>The Color Purple</u> (New York: Harcourt, 1982) 23.

² Alice Walker, <u>The Temple of My Familiar</u> (San Diego: Harcourt, 1989) 101.

Subsequent citations

³ Walker, <u>Temple</u> 34.

⁴ Walker, <u>Color Purple</u> 70-71.

The abbreviations *ibid.* (Latin *ibidem*, "in the same place") and *op. cit.* (Latin *opere citato*, "in the work cited") are no longer used with endnotes.

7b Endnote forms

On the following pages are endnote forms corresponding to the MLA Works Cited forms given in **3b**. A hypothetical page citation has been added to the end of each note to illustrate the positioning of page numbers in endnotes.

Table of endnote forms

Books

1. Book by one author
2. Book by two or more authors
3. Book by a committee, commission, association, or other group
4. Anonymous book
5. Later or revised edition of a book
6. Edited book (*author's work is being cited*)
7. Edited book (*editor's work is being cited*)
8. Translated book (*author's work is being cited*)
9. Translated book (*translator's work is being cited*)
10. Book in more than one volume
11. Republished book
12. Book that is part of a series
13. Book published by a division of a press
14. Book published before 1900
15. Book with incomplete publication information

Parts of books

16. Introduction, preface, foreword, or afterword in a book
17. Essay in a collection of essays by various authors
18. Poem, short story, or other work in an anthology
19. Journal or magazine article reprinted in a collection of essays by various authors

Articles in journals and magazines

20. Article in a journal paginated by the volume (*continuous pagination*)
21. Article in a journal paginated issue by issue
22. Article in a journal with issue numbers only
23. Article in a weekly or biweekly magazine
24. Article in a monthly or bimonthly magazine

Articles in newspapers

25. Article in a newspaper
26. Editorial in a newspaper
27. Letter to the editor

Other print sources

28. Abstract in *Dissertation Abstracts International*
29. Book review
30. Dissertation, unpublished
31. Encyclopedia article (*or article in similar reference work*)
32. Government document
33. Interview, published
34. Map
35. Pamphlet
36. Proceedings of a conference

Nonprint sources

37. Computer software
38. Film
39. Interview, personal
40. Lecture
41. Microfilm or microfiche
42. Recording
43. Television program
44. Videotape

Books

1. Book by one author

   [1] David Novarr, The Lines of Life: Theories of Biography, 1880–1970 (West Lafayette: Purdue UP, 1986) 113.

2. Book by two or more authors

   [2] Robert Scholes and Robert Kellogg, The Nature of Narrative (London: Oxford UP, 1966) 27.

3. **Book by a committee, commission, association, or other group**

³ Ground Zero, <u>Nuclear War: What's in It for You?</u>
(New York: Pocket, 1982) 66–67.

4. **Anonymous book**

⁴ <u>Kodak Guide to 35mm Photography</u> (Rochester:
Eastman Kodak, 1980) 12.

5. **Later or revised edition of a book**

⁵ Casey Miller and Kate Swift, <u>The Handbook of
Nonsexist Writing</u>, 2nd ed. (New York: Harper, 1988)
98.

6. **Edited book** (*author's work is being cited*)

⁶ Elizabeth Gaskell, <u>The Life of Charlotte
Brontë</u>, ed. Alan Shelston (Harmondsworth: Penguin,
1975) 254–55.

7. **Edited book** (*editor's work is being cited*)

⁷ Frederick Garber, ed., <u>The Italian</u>, by Ann
Radcliffe (London: Oxford UP, 1968) 201.

8. **Translated book** (*author's work is being cited*)

⁸ Ursula Brumm, <u>American Thought and Religious Typology</u>, trans. John Hoaglund (New Brunswick:
Rutgers UP, 1970) 107–08.

9. Translated book (*translator's work is being cited*)

⁹ L. R. Lind, trans., The Aeneid, by Vergil (Bloomington: Indiana UP, 1962) 76.

10. Book in more than one volume

¹⁰ Luigi Sturzo, Church and State, 2 vols. (Notre Dame: U of Notre Dame P, 1962) 1: 67.

11. Republished book

¹¹ William L. Shirer, Berlin Diary: The Journal of a Foreign Correspondent 1934–1941 (1941; Harmondsworth: Penguin 1979) 198.

12. Book that is part of a series

¹² Virginia L. Radley, Samuel Taylor Coleridge, Twayne's English Authors Ser. 36 (New York: Twayne, 1966) 34–36.

13. Book published by a division of a press

¹³ Barbara Ehrenreich and Deirdre English, For Her Own Good: 150 Years of the Experts' Advice to Women (Garden City: Anchor–Doubleday, 1979) 333.

14. Book published before 1900

¹⁴ Brainerd Kellogg, A Text-Book on Rhetoric (New York, 1897) 22.

15. Book with incomplete publication information

[15] George S. Marr, <u>The Periodical Essayists of the Eighteenth Century</u> (London: Clarke, n.d.) 40–44.

Parts of books

16. Introduction, preface, foreword, or afterword in a book

[16] J. Hillis Miller, introduction, <u>Bleak House</u>, by Charles Dickens, ed. Norman Page (Harmondsworth: Penguin, 1971) 12.

17. Essay in a collection of essays by various authors

[17] Richard E. Young, "Concepts of Art and the Teaching of Writing," <u>The Rhetorical Tradition and Modern Writing</u>, ed. James J. Murphy (New York: Modern Lang. Assn., 1982) 133.

18. Poem, short story, or other work in an anthology

[18] Walter Raleigh, "The Advice," <u>The Anchor Anthology of Sixteenth-Century Verse</u>, ed. Richard S. Sylvester (New York: Anchor–Doubleday, 1974) 330.

19. Journal or magazine article reprinted in a collection of essays by various authors

[19] Richard Harter Fogle, "The Abstractness of Shelley," <u>Philological Quarterly</u> 24 (1945): 362–79,

rpt. in Shelley: A Collection of Critical Essays,
ed. George M. Ridenour, Twentieth Century Views (Englewood Cliffs: Prentice, 1965) 28–29.

Articles in journals and magazines

20. Article in a journal paginated by the volume (*continuous pagination*)

[20] Jerome A. Miller, "Horror and the Deconstruction of the Self," Philosophy Today 32 (1988): 287.

21. Article in a journal paginated issue by issue

[21] George Butterick, "Charles Olson's 'The
Kingfishers' and the Poetics of Change," American
Poetry 6.2 (1989): 28–29.

22. Article in a journal with issue numbers only

[22] Paul Jacobson, "Temperature and Your Guitar's Health," Guitar Review 75 (1988): 17.

23. Article in a weekly or biweekly magazine

[23] Barbara Rudolph, "Adrift in the Doldrums,"
Time 31 July 1989: 33.

24. Article in a monthly or bimonthly magazine

[24] Mary Kay Blakely, "Coma: Stories from the
Edge of Death," Life Aug. 1989: 82.

Articles in newspapers
25. Article in a newspaper

[25] Denis Donoghue, "Does America Have a Major Poet?" New York Times 3 Dec. 1978, late city ed., sec. 7: 9.

26. Editorial in a newspaper

[26] "'Restraint' Spurs Terrorists," editorial, Chicago Sun-Times 3 Aug. 1989: 42.

27. Letter to the editor

[27] Lavonna Hayden, "Broadway Blues," letter, Village Voice 28 Feb. 1989: 4.

Other print sources
28. Abstract in *Dissertation Abstracts International*

[28] Susan Ellen Krantz, "The First Fortune: The Plays and the Playhouse," DAI 47 (1986): 189A (Tulane U).

29. Book review

[29] Norma Pettit, rev. of American Puritanism: Faith and Practice, by Darrett B. Rutman, New England Quarterly 43 (1970): 504-05.

30. Dissertation, unpublished

[30] James Vernon Rauff, "Machine Translation with Two-Level Grammars," diss., Northwestern U, 1988, 29.

31. Encyclopedia article

[31] "Phonetics," Encyclopaedia Britannica: Micropaedia, 15th ed., 1986.

32. Government document

[32] United States, Superintendent of Documents, Poetry and Literature (Washington: GPO, 1978) 7–8.

33. Interview, published

[33] Margaret Drabble, interview, Interviews with Contemporary Novelists, by Diana Cooper-Clark (New York: St. Martin's, 1986) 72–73.

34. Map

[34] Southeastern States, map (Falls Church: American Automobile Assn., 1988).

35. Pamphlet

[35] Dennison I. Rusinow, Yugoslavia's Muslim Nation (Hanover: Universities Field Staff Intl., 1982) 3.

36. Proceedings of a conference

[36] Stephen W. Rousseas, ed., Inflation: Its Causes, Consequences and Control, Symposium Held by the Dept. of Economics, New York U, 31 Jan. 1968 (Wilton: K. Kazanjian Economics Foundation, 1968) 77.

Nonprint sources
37. Computer software

[37] Thomas Etter and William Chamberlain, Racter, computer software, Mindscape, 1984.

38. Film

[38] Casablanca, dir. Michael Curtiz, with Humphrey Bogart, Ingrid Bergman, and Claude Rains, Warner Bros., 1942.

39. Interview, personal

[39] Teresa Toulouse, personal interview, 31 Mar. 1985.

40. Lecture

[40] James V. Catano, "The Paradox Behind the Myth of Self-Making: Self-Empowerment vs. the Power of the Academy," Conference on College Composition and Communication, Seattle, 17 Mar. 1989.

41. Microfilm or microfiche

When citing a publication reproduced on microfilm or microfiche, simply use the ordinary note form appropriate for that publication.

42. Recording

^{42} Fred W. Friendly and Walter Cronkite, eds.,
The Way It Was: The Sixties, narr. Walter Cronkite,
CBS, F3M 38858, 1983.

43. Television program

^{43} Nightline, ABC, WLS, Chicago, 23 Jan. 1990.

44. Videotape

^{44} The Beggar's Opera, videocassette, by John
Gay, prod. and dir. Jonathan Miller, with Roger Daltrey and Carol Hall, BBC-TV/RM Arts, 1985 (135 min.).

7c   Sample student paper

The student research paper that follows, Emmet Geary's "Recovery from the Florence Flood: A Masterpiece of Restoration," is an excellent example of an informative report that is tightly focused around a precise thesis statement. As explained in Chapter 1, Geary drew on his reading about the effects of the 1966 flood in Florence, Italy, to define a narrow subject for his paper—the efforts of professionals and volunteers to rescue and restore the city's valuable art. The thesis statement in which he introduces this focusing idea comes at the end of his first paragraph, a paragraph that compactly provides all the background needed by the reader to understand the rest of the paper.

Perhaps the best feature of this paper is Geary's skillful integration of his sources. A glance at his endnotes page shows that he has not relied too heavily on any one source; instead he moves back and forth among his sources, pulling together related pieces of information from different sources and weaving them into a coherent and well-developed narrative. Excellent transitions between paragraphs help to unify the paper, and Geary's clear explanations of occasionally technical information hold the reader's interest.

From start to finish, this paper is another example of the way in which the researcher's vision of his or her subject can shape the diverse products of reading and note taking into a unified and original whole.

Note the effective movement of Geary's introductory paragraph. It begins with a brief but specific survey of the flood's devastating impact on Florence, then moves to the damage done to the city's art, then (with the Batini quotation) shifts to the narrower subject of art restoration, the focus of Geary's paper.

Compare the version of the Batini quotation given in the paper with the original, on Geary's note card:

Batini, p. 90

"Despite the various complex restoration methods briefly explained above, the havoc played by the flood among works of art in Florence presented many new problems. For example, never before had so many and diverse works of art been damaged at the same time, all of which needed to be restored at once by an army of specialists, unfortunately a rarity today."

In Geary's paper, the bracketed capital *N* at the start of the quotation and the ellipses at the end indicate that only part of the original sentence is quoted here.

1/2"
1

Emmet Geary

Professor P. L. Herrold

History 100

March 28, 1990

Recovery from the Florence Flood:

A Masterpiece of Restoration

On November 4, 1966, the swollen Arno River in-
undated Florence, Italy. Nineteen inches of rain had
fallen in two days, causing floodwater to reach
depths of twenty feet in some parts of the city. The
damage was devastating: six thousand of the city's
ten thousand shops were destroyed, five thousand
families were left homeless, and more than a hundred
people drowned. But the primary reason that most out-
siders grieved for Florence was the damage to its
unique collection of Renaissance art treasures and
rare books. As Giorgio Batini noted, "[N]ever before
had so many and diverse works of art been damaged at
the same time, all of which needed to be restored at
once. . . ."[1] The story of this restoration is a
story of commitment and ingenuity. Though the Florence flood destroyed some priceless masterpieces
and heavily damaged others, it inspired valiant
efforts among professional restorers and untrained

If we compare Geary's paraphrase of Horton (note 3) with the original text, we see that he has effectively and accurately summarized the source in his own words:

A few days after the disastrous floods that occurred in Italy on November 4, 1966, a group of art lovers in the United States organized the Committee to Rescue Italian Art (CRIA). One of their first acts was to send, on November 8, two art historians to Florence and Venice, the areas where the art losses were reported to be the greatest, to assess the damage and to find out what could be done to help. Word was received from them by transatlantic telephone that restoration experts and materials were urgently needed. By November 14, there were 16 conservators on their way to Florence. Within the next week, they were joined by four more conservators. This group of 20, headed by Lawrence Majewski, acting director of the Conservation Center, Institute of Fine Arts, New York University, included: a chemist; 13 conservators of paintings, frescoes, mosaics, and furniture; two conservators of prints and drawings; one librarian; and three bookbinders, specializing in the restoration and conservation of books, manuscripts, and other library materials.

2

volunteers alike, and even occasioned some discover-
ies in the field of art that would otherwise never
have been made.

As the floodwater rose, the first demonstration
of dedication to art was shown by fourteen members
of the staff of the Uffizi Gallery, who risked their
lives to rescue twenty-four paintings stored in the
museum's basement.[2] When the floodwater had sub-
sided, generous contributions from all over the world
arrived in Florence, and hundreds of volunteers—
mainly students from throughout Europe and North
America—came to undertake the messy cleanup that
would return Florence to normal and salvage the
city's damaged treasures. The volunteers were led by
an international team of art historians and conservators. Within only a few days of the flood, for example, one group of American art lovers had organized
the Committee to Rescue Italian Art and two weeks
later had dispatched to Florence a team of twenty experts, including specialists in paintings, mosaics,
furniture, prints, bookbindings, and manuscripts.[3]

Two distinct types of damage to art had resulted
from the flood: that due to submersion, and that due
to water pressure, turbulence, and friction.

By inserting the citation to Ricci (note 5) in the middle of his sentence, Geary makes it clear that only the information in the first half of the sentence—the specific data about the size and speed of the floodwater—comes from this source.

Geary found his information about the damage to Ghiberti's baptistry doors in many sources; consequently, it could be considered common knowledge and did not require specific documentation.

3

Submersion caused the flood's most significant artistic loss--the great <u>Crucifix</u> by Giovanni Cimabue,
painted at the end of the thirteenth century--as well
as most of the other damage to paintings and books.
Compounding the problem of submersion was oil, which
had spilled from ruptured fuel tanks around the city,
and which rode the top of the floodwater, coating everything it touched. Having never before worked on
paintings stained by fuel oil, restorers were forced
to experiment with a number of solvents, including
benzene and carbon tetrachloride.[4] Water pressure
and turbulence created a different kind of devasta-
tion. Sweeping through the city at forty to fifty
miles an hour, the twelve-foot wave of water[5] knocked
sculptures from their pedestals and damaged the al-
tarpieces of churches. The famous baptistry doors
of the city's cathedral, cast by Lorenzo Ghiberti
in the fifteenth century, were violently battered
by the water, which dislodged five of the doors'
bronze panels.

The first task that restoration workers faced
was collecting the objects to be restored. Since the
last serious threat to Florence's art had come from
German artillery bombardment during World War II,

In his paragraph describing the flood's damage to Florence's libraries, note Geary's effective integration of related material from different sources.

A quotation of more than four typed lines is set off by indenting ten spaces. Double-space between the last line of the text and the first line of the quotation, and double-space the quotation itself. No quotation marks are used when a quotation is set off in this way.

4

many valuable books and manuscripts had been stored below ground for safety.[6] Now these books had to be pulled from library basements full of water and mud. In the Biblioteca Nazionale alone, more than 300,000 volumes were damaged; in the library of the Gabinetto Vieusseux, 250,000 more had been under water and needed immediate attention.[7] All told, nearly two million books were damaged by the flood.[8]

Not only the floodwater but the subsequent growth of destructive mold spores threatened Florence's priceless books. As Carolyn Horton explains, mold endangered even books that had escaped direct damage from the flood:

> Books are hygroscopic, i.e., have the capacity for absorbing water from the air around them. Therefore any books stored in conditions of high humidity are in danger of being damaged by mold. We had received reports that the flooded area of Florence had become, in effect, a huge humidity chamber. The wet books in rooms that were ony partially flooded were humidifying the dry books on the upper shelves.[9]

Again, the information given here about methods of restoring and drying books was available in several sources and therefore did not require documentation in Geary's paper.

Note Geary's smooth transition between the last two paragraphs, which deal with salvaging books, and this one, which moves on to consider damage done to paintings on wooden panels: "Like books. . . ."

Compare Geary's version of the quotation from the anonymous article "The Florentine Flood Disaster" (note 10) with the original text:

> The situation regarding panel paintings has not changed much since the preliminary reports. The return to health will be slow and laborious. As is well known, when the water has soaked into the wood, the priming layer of glue and gesso dissolves, and the colours dissolve with it. This is not only the case with panels that were entirely submerged, as at Santa Croce (Fig. I). Even in cases where a few inches along the bottom were submerged, those parts buckle, and crack the part that seemed safe. More unexpected still, some panels which seemed quite undamaged when the flood subsided, developed blisters two or three days later, and the paint began to fall.

Note the editorial changes that Geary has made: (1) he has enclosed the initial *W* of his quotation in brackets to indicate that the first words of the original quotation have been omitted; (2) he has inserted the word *plaster* in brackets to define the unfamiliar term *gesso* for the reader; (3) he has inserted ellipsis marks to indicate an omission after his third sentence (note that the usual three periods follow a fourth period—the period of the sentence); and (4) he has inserted the word *only* in brackets to make the sense of the original quotation clearer. Geary has retained the unorthodox punctuation and the British spelling ("colours") of the original text.

5

Salvaged books, covered with mud and oil and soaked
with water, were first washed with mild soap and then
treated with fungicides and antibiotics that would
inhibit the growth of mold and bacteria. Then came
the drying, by any means available: heating in to-
bacco ovens and brick kilns, interleaving pages with
absorbent paper, spraying with powder.

Like books, paintings on wooden panels were particularly susceptible to damage from submersion in
water. As one observer described the problem:

> [W]hen the water has soaked into the wood,
> the priming layer of glue and gesso [plas-
> ter] dissolves, and the colours dissolve
> with it. . . . Even in cases where [only]
> a few inches along the bottom were sub-
> merged, those parts buckle, and crack the
> part that seemed safe. More unexpected
> still, some panels which seemed quite un-
> damaged when the flood subsided, devel-
> oped blisters two or three days later, and
> the paint began to fall.[10]

To prevent wooden panels from drying too fast and
shrinking, thus causing the pigment to flake off,
restoration workers had to reduce the humidity around

Another excellent transition links these two paragraphs: "Even more difficult to restore. . . ."

the panels gradually. Within twelve days of the
flood, the Limonaia, a large greenhouse in one of
Florence's public parks, was converted to a sophisticated drying facility complete with an elaborate
humidity-control system. Initially set at ninety
percent, the humidity level inside was gradually low-
ered, and the panels were constantly checked to
ensure sufficiently slow drying.[11] Only after complete drying, a process that sometimes took many
months, could the painted panels be moved to labora-
tories for further restoration, which usually involved planing down the back of the panels until only
the pigment and priming layers remained, and then
attaching a laminated, shrink-proof panel to the
back of the painting.[12]

Even more difficult to restore were Florence's
frescoes, paintings originally executed directly on
damp plaster, so that the pigment fused with the surface of the wall. Besides damage from submersion and
floating fuel oil, frescoes were affected by dampness, which caused the plaster layers to separate
from the wall,[13] and by salt contained in the floodwater, which penetrated the plaster and caused "tiny
explosions" in the painted surface as the wall

When parts of a sentence derive from different sources, insert references to the appropriate notes in midsentence, as Geary has done here, for accurate documentation. Consider the following two note cards.

"Florentine Flood Disaster," p. 193

Damage to frescoes more serious than people thought at first: dampness penetrated plaster even above the level of the floodwater, causing [4] "a breaking down of the adhesion between the plaster layers and the wall."

"Slow Art Restoration," p. 42

Salt dissolved in the floodwaters "had become lodged inside and under wood panels and frescoes, causing tiny explosions to tear the paint."

7

dried.[14] To save frescoes, restorers used a technique called "strapo," which involves applying a
coating of glue and a canvas sheet to the wall. After
the glue has dried, the painting can be pulled from
the wall intact on the canvas. Difficult as this process is, it yielded an unexpected reward: when the
painted surfaces were removed, more than three hundred sinopias, or preliminary drawings for the frescoes, were uncovered on the walls.[15]

Surprisingly, sculpture seems to have received
more benefit than harm from the flood. Some statues
were actually cleaned by the swirling water, whose
mud acted as a gentle abrasive, removing the grime
of hundreds of years. The restorers themselves used
mud to clean sections of statues that were untouched
by the floodwater.[16] Fuel oil, on the other hand,
did pose a serious threat to sculpture. Since marble
is a porous stone, the oil penetrated beneath the
surface and had to be drawn out and absorbed by
talc applied to the statues. But such thorough
cleaning of these statues actually left them cleaner
than they had been before the flood and led to a few
surprises. For example, the restoration revealed
for the first time that Donatello's statue The Magda-

The Ricci quotation provides the foundation for an effective concluding paragraph. It not only echoes ideas from the paper's introduction but also gives Geary the opportunity to reiterate one of his main ideas— the importance of the volunteer efforts to save Florence's art.

8

<u>len</u> had originally had gilded hair.[17]

Only a few months after the floodwater had devastated Florence, as the frantic restoration work continued, Leonardo Ricci aptly described the world's reaction to the disaster. "Many floods indeed and natural tragedies have happened everywhere in the world," he wrote. "But never have we heard such a cry as for Florence. As if, instead of a city it were a person, a loved one who in a way belongs to everybody and without whom it is impossible to live."[18] In a real sense, the rescued art of Florence does belong to everyone: without generous contributions of money from around the world and the tireless efforts of an international corps of volunteers, Florence's treasures could not have survived.

One hallmark of a successful research paper is the writer's ability to integrate his or her sources—that is, to avoid dependence on a single source for large sections of the paper and to draw instead from many different sources as he or she composes. A glance at the sequence of Geary's notes shows how well he has integrated material from his research.

Subsequent references to a source for which full publication information has been given consist only of the author's last name and the page number. Do not use the abbreviations *ibid.* and *op. cit.*

The March 12, 1967, issue of the *New York Times* is a Sunday edition divided into sections; the section number must therefore be included in the citation. The August 9, 1967, issue—a weekday issue—is paged continuously without section divisions; no section number is necessary, since there is only one page 42 in the issue.

Notes

[1] Giorgio Batini, 4 November 1966: The River Arno in the Museums of Florence, trans. Timothy Paterson (Florence: Bonechi Editore, 1967) 90.

[2] Eric Rhode, "Good News from Florence," New Statesman 6 Jan. 1967: 20.

[3] Carolyn Horton, "Saving the Libraries of Florence," Wilson Library Bulletin 41 (1967): 1035.

[4] Joseph Judge, "Florence Rises from the Flood," National Geographic July 1967: 39.

[5] Leonard Ricci, "Exploratory Research in Urban Form and the Future of Florence," Arts and Architecture Feb. 1967: 25.

[6] Horton 1036.

[7] "The Florentine Flood Disaster," Burlington Magazine 109 (1967): 194.

[8] Horton 1036.

[9] Horton 1035.

[10] "Florentine Flood Disaster" 193.

[11] Batini 90–91.

[12] "Road Back is Long for Florentines," New York Times 12 Mar. 1967, late city ed., sec. 1: 80.

[13] "Florentine Flood Disaster" 193.

Ricci's article begins on page 25 but continues on nonconsecutive pages later in the magazine.

10

[14] "Slow Art Restoration Continues in Florence," <u>New York Times</u> 9 Aug. 1967, late city ed.: 42.

[15] "Church Found Under Basilica in Florence,"
<u>New York Times</u> 4 Nov. 1967, late city ed.: 35.

[16] Batini 103–05

[17] "Florentine Flood Disaster" 194.

[18] Ricci 25, 32.

Mechanics

The appearance of a paper, like the appearance of a person, indicates regard for self and for the world at large. Accurate typing, a clean page, observance of editing conventions—all of these suggest a writer's confidence and authority. Wise writers use any available means—including care with mechanics—to win the favor and attention of their readers.

8a Manuscript preparation

Unless your instructor specifies otherwise, you should prepare your essays on standard 8½-by-11-inch white paper. Typed papers—which are preferable—should be double-spaced on unruled white bond. If your instructor permits handwritten papers, use wide-ruled paper, write legibly in black or dark blue ink, and skip lines. An instructor or an editor grows weary with a manuscript that has to be puzzled out one word at a time. Give your thoughts and sentences a fair chance by presenting them neatly on the page.

1. Format

Below are some widely accepted conventions for arranging the text on your page. Your instructor may have additional, or different, requirements.

1. Type or write on one side of the sheet only.
2. Leave a margin of one inch on the top, bottom, and sides of typed papers, slightly more for handwritten essays.
3. On four double-spaced lines in the upper left corner of the first page, give your name, your instructor's name, the course number,

and the date. Double-space again (or skip another line) and center your title. Do not use quotation marks or underline your title unless it includes words that require such punctuation (see **8e**). Capitalize all words in the title except articles, short conjunctions, and short prepositions. Double-space after your title and begin the first line of your essay.

4. Indent paragraphs five spaces when you type. In handwritten manuscripts, indent about an inch.
5. Number all pages with Arabic numbers in the upper right corner, one-half inch from the top of the page.

2. Quotations

When you reproduce quotations in your text, observe the following conventions. (For an extended discussion of the correct use of quotations, see **4c**.)

1. A quotation of only a few words should be incorporated into your sentences:

> In Childhood and Society, Erik Erikson notes that
>
> the young adult, "emerging from the search for
>
> and insistence on identity," has become "ready
>
> for intimacy."

2. A quotation of more than four typed lines of prose, or more than three lines of verse, should be set off from the main text without quotation marks by indenting. Introduce the quotation with a colon unless the quotation begins in the middle of a sentence that grammatically continues your own sentence of introduction; in that case, use no punctuation. Indent the quotation ten spaces from the left margin, double-spacing between the last line of your text and the first line of the quotation, and between the lines of the quotation itself.
3. A quotation of poetry should be divided into lines exactly as the original is divided. If an entire line of verse does not fit on one

line of the page, the words left over should be indented on the next line:

> Allons! the inducements shall be greater,
>
> We will sail pathless and wild seas,
>
> We will go where winds blow, waves dash,
>
>> and the Yankee clipper speeds by
>>
>> under full sail.

4. When quoting dialogue from a story, novel, or play, be sure to reproduce the paragraphing and punctuation of the quotation exactly as in the original.

> "Are you better, Minet—Chéri?"
>
> "Yes. I can't think what came over me."
>
> The grey eyes, gradually reassured, dwelt on mine.
>
> "I think I know what it was. A smart little rap on the knuckles from Above."
>
> I remained pale and troubled and my mother misunderstood:
>
> "There, there now. There's nothing so terrible as all that in the birth of a child, nothing terrible at all. It's much more beautiful in real life. The suffer—ing is so quickly forgotten, you'll see! The proof that all women forget is that it is only men——and what business was it of

```
Zola's, anyway?--who write stories about

it."
```

Note, incidentally, that British writers and publishers commonly use a single quotation mark (') where American convention requires double quotation marks(").

3. Manuscript corrections

If a reading of your final draft shows the need for minor corrections, make them unmistakably clear. It is not necessary to recopy an entire page for the sake of one or two small insertions or alterations, but recopying is called for if the number of corrections would make the page difficult to read or messy in appearance. Words to be inserted should be typed or written above the line, and their proper position should be indicated by a caret (ʌ) placed below the line.

```
      other
On the hand, Nightingale's books on the nursing pro-
        ʌ
fession remained influential for years after her

death.
```

Inserted words should not be enclosed in parentheses or brackets unless these marks are required by the sentence. Cancel words by drawing a neat line through them, not by enclosing them in parentheses or brackets.

8b Capital letters

The general principle governing capitalization is that proper nouns are capitalized and common nouns are not. A proper noun is the name of a particular person, place, or thing:

Richard Wright	Alaska	the Capitol
Virginia Woolf	New Orleans	the Golden Gate Bridge

A common noun is a more general term that can be used as a name for a number of persons, places, or things:

author	state	building
woman	city	bridge

Note that the same word may be used as both a proper and a common noun.

> Of all the *peaks* in the Rocky Mountains, *Pike's Peak* is the mountain I would most like to climb.

> Our beginning *history* class studied *legislative* procedure and the part our *representatives* play in it. When I took *History 27,* our class visited the *Legislative* Committee hearing in which *Representative* Cella expressed his views on the Alliance for Progress.

Abbreviations are capitalized when the words they stand for would be capitalized: USN, ROTC, NBC.

1. Proper nouns

Capitalize proper nouns and adjectives derived from them. Proper nouns include the following:

1. Days of the week, months, and holidays:

Sunday	Thanksgiving
October	New Year's Eve

2. Organizations such as political parties, governmental bodies and departments, societies, institutions, clubs, churches, and corporations:

Socialist Party	Boston Public Library
U.S. Senate	Optimist's Club
Department of the Interior	Greek Orthodox Church
American Cancer Society	Raytheon Company

3. Members of organizations:

Republicans	Buddhists
Lions	Girl Scouts

4. Historical events, periods, and documents:

    Battle of Hastings   Declaration of Independence

    Middle Ages   Stamp Act

    Baroque Era   Magna Carta

5. Specific places and geographical areas:

    Latin America   Colorado River

    Ellis Island   the Far East

    Sahara Desert   the Midwest

6. Names of races, ethnic groups, and languages (but not the words *white* and *black* when used to refer to races):

    Caucasian   Japanese

    African-American   Italian

7. Names of religions, religious figures and holidays, and sacred books:

    the Lord   the Bible

    the Son of God   the Book of Mormon

    Allah   Day of Atonement

    Lutheran   All Saints' Day

8. Registered trademarks:

    Coca-Cola   Volvo

    Tide   Sony

9. Terms identifying family members only when such words are used in place of proper names:

    My sister and brother both received letters from Grandmother and Grandpa.

10. Titles of persons when they precede proper names. When titles are used without proper names, only those of high rank should be capitalized:

    Senator Marsh   Professor Stein   Aunt Elsa

    Both the Governor and the Attorney General endorsed the candidacy of our representative.

    The postmaster of our town appealed to the Postmaster General.

11. In biological nomenclature, the names of genera but not of species:

    Homo sapiens   *Equus caballus*
    Salmo irideus   *Aquila heliaca*

12. Stars, constellations, and planets, but not the words *earth, sun,* or *moon* unless they are used as astronomical names:

    Sirius   Taurus
    Arcturus   Jupiter

2. Titles of works

Capitalize the first word and the important words of the titles of books, plays, articles, musical compositions, pictures, and other literary or artistic works. Unimportant words in a title are the articles *a, an,* and *the;* short conjunctions; and short prepositions.

> *I, Claudius   Summer in Williamsburg*   Beethoven's *Third Symphony*
> *Childhood and Society   Measure for Measure   Friar Felix at Large*
> Brancusi's "Bird in Space"   Bruce Springsteen's "Born in the U.S.A."

3. Sentences and quotations

Capitalize the first word of every sentence and of every direct quotation in dialogue. Note that a capital letter is not used for the part of a quotation that follows an interpolated expression like *he said,* unless that expression begins a new sentence.

> "Mow the lawn diagonally," said Mrs. Grant, "and go over it twice."
> "Mow the lawn twice diagonally," said Mrs. Grant. "It will be even smoother if the second mowing crosses over the first one."
> Mrs. Grant said, "Mow the lawn twice."

Following a colon, the first words in a series of short questions or sentences may be capitalized.

> The first-aid questions were dull but important: What are the first signs of shock in accident victims? Should they be kept warm? Should they eat? Should they drink?

Capitalize the first word of every line of poetry except when the poem itself does not use a capital letter.

> I'll walk where my own nature would be leading:
>> It vexes me to choose another guide:
> Where the grey flocks in ferny glens are feeding;
>> Where the wild wind blows on the mountain-side.
>
> —Emily Brontë

> last night i heard
> a pseudobird;
> or possibly
> the usual bird
> heard pseudome.
>> —Ebenezer Peabody

8c Numbers

In general, treat all numbers in a particular context similarly; in the interest of consistency, do not use words for some and figures for others. The following additional guidelines for writing numbers are widely accepted.

1. Numbers from one to ten and round numbers that can be expressed in one or two words are usually written out.

   three people in line

   twenty-five flavors

   seven hundred reserved seats

Adjectival forms of numbers are also written out when they can be expressed in one or two words.

   second chance

   thirty-fifth floor

   the *ten-thousandth* customer

All numbers that begin a sentence are written out, even though they would ordinarily be represented by figures.

   Four hundred sixty dollars was too much.

2. To indicate a range of numbers, use the complete second number up to 99.

    33–34   90–99

For larger numbers, use the last two digits of the second number unless more are required.

    123–25   100–09
    399–401   12,500–13,000

3. Use figures to express the day of the month and the year in a date.

    December 7, 1941   14 July 1789

References to centuries and decades are usually written out in lowercase letters but may be expressed in figures. In the latter case, the figures are followed by an *s* without an apostrophe.

    the *nineteenth* century   the 1800s
    the *sixties*   the 1960s, the '60s

Write out the names of centuries when they are used as adjectives.

    a *twentieth*-century invention

4. Use figures for numbers in street addresses; long numbers; chapter and page numbers; time citations followed directly by *A.M.* or *P.M.*; and decimals.

    525 Spring Street   page 33
    11337 Palm Boulevard   9:00 P.M. [but *nine o'clock*]
    1,275 gallons   7:25 A.M.
    Chapter 12   8.5 percent

Use figures with abbreviations and symbols.

    80 lbs.   66%
    55 mph   6'1"

5. Use figures after a dollar sign.

    $12.50 $1,000

If the amount of money in question can be expressed in one or two words, it may be written out.

fifty-five cents   *sixteen* dollars

Amounts of money in the millions, billions, or trillions of dollars may be expressed with a combination of figures and words when a dollar sign is used.

$12 million (but *twelve million dollars*)

8d Abbreviations

Minimize the use of abbreviations in expository prose. As a general rule, spell out the first names of people, the words in addresses (*North, Street, New Jersey*), the days of the week and the months of the year, and units of measurement (*ounces, pounds, kilometers, hours, quarts*).

Elliott Brodie of 327 *West* 27th *Avenue*, Kenosha, *Wisconsin*, died on *December* 16, 1989.

Abbreviations cannot be avoided entirely, however, and it is important to be familiar with the most important conventions governing their use.

1. Some abbreviations are always written with periods.

Mr.	Ph.D.
etc.	i.e.
A.D.	P.M.

Others, such as the U.S. Postal Service abbreviations for states and the abbreviations for many organizations and agencies, are written without periods.

CA	DAR
TX	FAA

Acronyms (abbreviations spoken as words) are also written without periods.

NATO	UNICEF
MADD	OPEC

Still other abbreviations may be written with or without periods.

mph or m.p.h.	USA or U.S.A.
rpm or r.p.m.	PTA or P.T.A.

Your best guide to the proper punctuation of an abbreviation is a good desk dictionary. Many such dictionaries conveniently collect all abbreviations in a separate appendix.

2. Civil, religious, military, and academic titles are usually written out.

Senator Kennedy	Governor Cuomo
Secretary Baker	Colonel Mason
Father O'Malley	Professor Meyer

Such titles may be abbreviated only when they are followed by a person's full name: *Sen. Edward Kennedy,* but not *Sen. Kennedy.* The titles *Reverend* and *Honorable* must be followed by a full name *and* preceded by the word *the.*

the Reverend Thomas Jones (not *the Reverend Jones*)

the Honorable Alice Simpson (not *the Honorable Simpson*)

The word *the* is dropped if these titles are abbreviated, but the abbreviated forms must also be followed by a full name.

Rev. Thomas Jones (not *Rev. Jones*)

Hon. Alice Simpson (not *Hon. Simpson*)

3. The titles below are abbreviated when they precede names.

Mr.	Mrs.
Messrs.	Dr.
Ms.	St. [Saint]

Titles and degrees such as the following are also abbreviated after names.

Sr.	Ph.D.
Jr.	M.A.
M.D.	LL.D.
D.D.S.	Esq.

Do not duplicate a title before *and* after a name.

Incorrect   Dr. Rinard Z. Hart, *M.D.*

Correct   Rinard Z. Hart, *M.D.*, or
Dr. Rinard Z. Hart

4. The words *volume, chapter, edition,* and *page* should be written out in references within a text, but abbreviated in parenthetical citations and bibliographies.

I found this quotation on *page* 267 of the third *edition.*

For further information on proper terms for addressing dignitaries, consult the Appendix of your style manual (*pp.* 664–80).

5. In technical writing, directions, recipes, and the like, terms of measurement are often abbreviated when used with figures.

32° F	½ tsp.
5 cc	32 mpg
12 ft.	4 hrs

6. When referring to corporations, use the ampersand (&) and abbreviations such as *Co., Inc.,* and *Bros.* only when a company uses such an abbreviation in its official title.

Incorrect   D.C. Heath & Co.

Correct   D. C. Heath and Company

7. Abbreviations that end in a period form their plurals by adding *-'s.*

two *Ph.D.'s*   *M.A.'s* in several disciplines

Abbreviations that do not end in a period usually form their plurals by adding *-s* without an apostrophe.

the *PTAs* of both schools

a fraternity house full of *BMOCs*

8e Italics

Italics are used for certain titles, unnaturalized foreign words, scientific names, names of ships and aircraft, and words used as words.

To italicize a word in a manuscript, draw one straight line below it, or use the underlining key on the keyboard: <u>King Lear.</u>

1. Italicize all words in the titles of books and monographs; plays and motion pictures; magazines, journals, and newspapers; paintings and sculpture; and long poems and long musical compositions. The article *the* preceding the title of a newspaper is not italicized or capitalized.

> Stephen Crane's *The Red Badge of Courage*
>
> Arthur Miller's *Death of a Salesman*
>
> *The Wizard of Oz*
>
> *Newsweek*
>
> the *Southern Review*
>
> the *Chicago Tribune*
>
> the *Mona Lisa*
>
> Michelangelo's *David*
>
> Alexander Pope's *The Rape of the Lock*
>
> Ravel's *Bolero*

Titles of parts of published works and articles in magazines are enclosed in quotation marks.

> The assignment is "Despondency" from William Wordsworth's long narrative poem, *The Excursion.*
>
> In the *New Yorker,* I always read filler material entitled "Letters We Never Finished Reading."
>
> She hoped to publish her story entitled "Nobody Lives Here" in a magazine like *Harper's.*

2. Italicize foreign words that have not yet become accepted in the English language. If you are not certain whether a foreign word has become naturalized, consult a dictionary. Be sure to consult the dictionary's explanatory notes to see how foreign words are indicated. Italicize the Latin scientific names for plants and animals.

A feeling of *gemütlichkeit* pervaded the hotel we stayed at in Munich.

The technical name of Steller's jay is *Cyanocitta stelleri.*

3. Italicize the names of ships, planes, trains, and spacecraft.

The S.S. *Constitution* sails for Africa tomorrow.

We saw Lindbergh's *Spirit of St. Louis* when we visited Washington last month.

I'm going to Baltimore on Amtrak's *Yankee Clipper.*

Voyager 2 is still sending back information from deep space.

8f   Syllabication

Dividing a word at the end of a line is mainly a printer's problem. In manuscripts it is not necessary to keep the right-hand margin absolutely even, so it is seldom necessary to divide a word at the end of a line. If such a division is essential, observe the following principles, and mark the division with a hyphen (-).

1. Divide words only *between* syllables—that is, between the normal sound divisions of a word. When in doubt as to where the division between syllables comes, consult a dictionary. One-syllable words, such as *though* or *strength,* cannot be divided. Syllables of one letter should not be divided from the rest of the word. Nor should a division be made between two letters that indicate a single sound. For example, never divide *th* as in *brother, sh* as in *fashion, ck* as in *Kentucky, oa* as in *reproaching,* or *ai* as in *maintain.* Such combinations of letters may be divided only if they indicate two distinct sounds: *post-haste, dis-hon-or, co-au-thor.*

> **Incorrect**   a-dult, burg-lar-ize, co-ord-in-a-tion, li-mit, ver-y
>
> **Correct**   adult, bur-glar-ize, co-or-di-na-tion, lim-it, very

2. A division usually comes at the point where a prefix or suffix joins the root word.

> anti-dote, be-half, con-vene, de-tract, sub-way
>
> fall-en, Flem-ish, lik-able (or like-able), like-ly, place-ment,
>   tall-er, tall-est

This rule does not hold when it contradicts the normal pronunciation of the word.

> bus-tling, jog-gled, prej-u-dice, prel-ate, res-ti-tu-tion, twin-kling

3. When two consonants come between vowels (me*mb*er), the division is between the consonants if pronunciation permits (*mem-ber*). If the consonant is doubled before a suffix, the second consonant goes with the suffix (*plan-ning*).

> at-tend, bur-lesque, clas-sic, dif-fer, fas-ten, fit-ting, hin-der, im-por-tant, laun-der, nar-rate, pas-sage, rab-bit, rum-mage, ser-geant, ten-don
> BUT NOTE: knowl-edge

4. The division comes after a vowel if pronunciation permits.

> devi-ate, modi-fier, ora-torical, oscilla-tor

EXERCISE 1

Correct any errors in capitalization, numbers, abbreviations, and italics.

1. The 1st bridges on the Earth were natural ones, formed by rocks and fallen trees.
2. The romans built incredible bridges out of rocks and concrete—some still stand 1,000 yrs. later.
3. Many bridges were built by 12th-century christians who wanted to carry their message all over europe.
4. According to the book Great Bridges of the World, bridge building, already sophisticated in many ways, became a Science in the seventeen hundreds.
5. Iron was introduced in bridges in seventeen seventy-nine, and in the last ½ of the 19 cent. bridge-builders began using steel.
6. There are 4 main kinds of bridges—beam, arch, suspension, and canti-lever—and 2 types of moveable bridges, pivot and vertical lift, which are a far cry from the drawbridges of Medieval Times.
7. The longest cantilever bridge, 3,239 ft. overall, is the quebec bridge over the saint lawrence river in Canada.
8. The lake pontchartrain causeway in La., called the longest bridge in the world, is 23.87 mi. long.
9. Bridges are technically fascinating, but a person doesn't have to be a Prof. of Engineering to appreciate their beauty.
10. Many bridges—such as the golden gate bridge in San Francisco, CA, and the famous london bridge, which was dismantled and moved to Ariz.—are Tourist attractions.

EXERCISE 2

Correct any errors in capitalization, numbers, abbreviations, and italics.

1. Because movies are a reliable gauge of the Country's social attitudes, analyzing images of native americans in films can reveal a great deal.
2. Early images of native americans were of Savages, 100s of Godless warmongers who attacked small groups of innocent Settlers, and an occasional indian who recognized the value of the White Man's ways.
3. In some movies, at least a few of the Whites were equally bad, stealing land and carrying off indian women, but the larger evils of Government exploitation and genocide were never suggested.
4. One of the 1st movies to break this trend was Broken Arrow, which appeared in nineteen fifty.
5. In the 1957 movie Run of the Arrow, Rod Steiger played an outcast who considered becoming a sioux, but became an american citizen instead.
6. Over the next 15 yrs., movies began to recognize the existence of nat. am. cultures beyond the stereotypical tepees and peace pipes.
7. For ex., eighty % of the dialogue in A Man called Horse is in sioux.
8. It was not until Little big man in 1970 that a native american, chief Dan George, was cast in a lead role in a major motion picture.
9. The nineteen-eighty film Windwalker also stands out; even though a Brit. actor played the lead, the entire movie was done in the cheyenne and crow languages, with subtitles in english.
10. Perhaps these changes indicate that Mainstream American Culture is recognizing that the role of native americans in this country transcends cowboy-and-indian games.

Index

abbreviation
  in bibliography, 205
  in citation, 205
  with figures, 205
  period with, 203
  plural of, 205
  of title, 204–5
abstract, dissertation
  endnote citation of, 169
  MLA citation of, 50
abstract page, APA form for, 134
  sample, 137
acronym, 203
ampersand, 205
anthology
  endnote citation of, 167
  MLA citation of, 47
anthropology, reference works for,
  23–24
APA documentation
  characteristics of, 112–13
  sample research paper illustrating,
  135–59
APA paper format, 132–34
APA reference forms, 113–25

APA source citation, 125–32
architecture, reference works for, 17
art
  APA citation of, 124–25
  reference works for, 17
article (written)
  APA citation of, 119–21
  endnote citation of, 167–69
  MLA citation of, 47–50
atlas, 17
audiotape, APA citation of, 124–25
authority, of sources for research,
  60–61

bibliography, working, 37–39
bibliography page, 161
bibliography, reference works for,
  17–18
book
  APA citation of, 115–18
  endnote citation of, 164–67
  italics with title of, 206
  MLA citation of, 50
book part
  APA citation of, 118–19

book part (*continued*)
  endnote citation of, 167
  MLA citation of, 46–47
book review
  APA citation of, 121–22
  endnote citation of, 169
  MLA citation of, 50
brackets, 56, 106, 152

capitalization, 197–201
  of proper nouns, 198–200
  of sentences and quotations, 200–201
  of titles of works, 200
card catalog, 13–16
caret, 197
CD-ROM data-base search, 31–34
chart, APA citation of, 124–25
classics, reference works for, 18
colon
  capitalization after, 200
  introducing long quotation with, 79, 108, 126
commerce, reference works for, 19
common knowledge, plagiarism vs., 76–77
common noun, 197–98
computer software
  APA citation of, 124
  endnote citation of, 171
  MLA citation of, 53
conference, proceedings of
  APA citation of, 123–24
  endnote citation of, 171
  MLA citation of, 52–53
content note, 86–87, 110, 134, 144, 159
currency, of sources for research, 60
current events, reference works for, 18

dance, reference works for, 21
data-base search
  CD-ROM, 31–34
  on-line, 29–31
Dewey Decimal System, 15
dialogue
  capitalization with, 200
  quoting, 196–97
direct quotation
  accuracy of, 73
  capitalization in, 200–201
  citation of, in research paper, 79–84, 126–31
  manuscript form for, 195–97
  in notes, 56
dissertation
  APA citation of, 122
  endnote citation of, 170
  MLA citation of, 51
documenting sources, in research paper
  in APA style, 112–13, 125–32
  in endnote style, 160–62
  in MLA style, 77–87
dollar sign, 203

economics, reference works for, 19
education, reference works for, 19
ellipses, 56, 96, 106, 142, 174
encyclopedia
  APA citation of, 122–23
  endnote citation of, 170
  MLA citation of, 51
endnotes, 160–93
  citation forms in, 162–72
  features of, 161
  page, 161–62
  sample research paper
    documented with, 172–93
essay
  APA citation of, 118–19

endnote citation of, 167
MLA citation of, 46
Essay and General Literature Index,
28–29

film
APA citation of, 124–25
endnote citation of, 171
MLA citation of, 53
reference works for, 19
footnote, 160
in APA documentation, 134, 144,
159
foreign words, italics with, 206

gazetteer, 17
general reference works, 17
government document, 34–35
APA citation of, 123
endnote citation of, 170
MLA citation of, 51

history, reference works for, 19–
20
hyphen, with syllabication, 207–8

ibid., 162
interview
APA citation of, 123
endnote citation of, 170, 171
MLA citation of, 52, 53
italics, 205–7
added to quotation for emphasis,
146–47

journal (published)
APA citation of, 119–20
endnote citation of, 168
MLA citation of, 47–48

lecture
APA citation of, 125
endnote citation of, 171
MLA citation of, 53
library
card catalog in, 13–16
data-base searches in, 29–34
Essay and General Literature Index,
28–29
government documents in, 34–35
locating books in, 15
on-line catalog in, 15–16
periodical indexes in, 24–28
reference works in, 23–24
Library of Congress System, 15
literature, reference works for, 20–
21

magazine
APA citation of, 120
endnote citation of, 168
MLA citation of, 48–49
manuscript
corrections in, 197
format of, 194–95
quotation in, 195–97
map
endnote citation of, 170
MLA citation of, 52
microfilm or microfiche
endnote citation of, 172
MLA citation of, 54
MLA documentation
characteristics of, 77–78
sample research paper illustrating,
93–111
MLA paper format, 87–88
MLA source citation, 77–87
MLA Works Cited forms, 39–54
music, reference works for, 21

214 *Index*

APA citation of, 121
endnote citation of, 169
MLA citation of, 49–50
note card, 55–56, 174, 186
notes
content, 86–87, 110, 134, 144,
159
identifying connections among,
69–70
note cards, 55–56, 174, 186
organizing, 70–71
selectivity in taking, 59–60
types of, 56–58
noun
common, 197–98
proper, 197–200
numbers, writing out, 201–3

objectivity, of sources for research,
61
on-line catalog, 15–16
on-line data-base search, 29–31
op. cit., 162
outline, for research paper, 71

pamphlet
endnote citation of, 170
MLA citation of, 52
paraphrase, 58, 176
accuracy of, 75–76
APA citation of, 131–32
MLA citation of, 84–86
period, with abbreviation, 203
periodical index, 24–28
philosophy, reference works for, 21
plagiarism, 11, 56, 58
avoiding, 72–77
political science, reference works for,
22

proceedings of a conference
APA citation of, 123–24
endnote citation of, 171
MLA citation of, 52–53
proper noun, 197–200
psychology, reference works for, 22

quotation
accuracy of, 73–74
APA citation of, 126–31
capitalization in, 200–201
direct. *See* direct quotation
long, 79
in manuscript, 195–97
MLA citation of, 79–84
in notes, 56
quotation marks, 73–74, 195
title in, 206

reader, of research paper, 9–10
recording
endnote citation of, 172
MLA citation of, 54
reference list, APA
characteristics of, 112–13
citation forms in, 113–25
format of, 134
sample, 157–58
reference works, 16–24
religion, reference works for, 22
report, 2–4. *See also* research paper
APA citation of, 124
research
identifying subject for, 7–9
preparing for, 2–7
recursiveness of, 12
understanding of, 11–12
research paper
APA documentation of, 112–
32

APA format for, 132–34
assessing subject for, 61–62
considering reader of, 9–10
endnote documentation of, 160–72
features of, 6–7
finding subject for, 7–9
MLA documentation of, 39–54, 77–87
MLA format for, 87–88
notes for, 55–60, 69–71
organization of, 68–71
outline of, 71
paraphrasing in, 75–76
plagiarism in, 72–77
planning, 10–12
quoting in, 73–74
revision of, 72
sample, APA documentation, 135–59
sample, endnote documentation, 175–93
sample, MLA documentation, 93–111
sources of information for. *See* source, for research paper
subheadings in, 140
title page of, 88, 133
types of, 2–6
working bibliography for, 37–39
writing, 71–72
researched argument, 4–6
review
APA citation of, 121–22
endnote citation of, 169
MLA citation of, 50

sciences, reference works for, 23
sentence, capitalization in, 200–201

single quotation marks, 197
slash, 98
slides, APA citation of, 124–25
sociology, reference works for, 23–24
software
APA citation of, 124
endnote citation of, 171
MLA citation of, 53
source, for research paper
assessing quality and appropriateness of, 60–61
books as, 13–16, 28–29
citing, APA style, 112–13, 125–32
citing, endnote style, 160–62
citing, MLA style, 77–87
in data base, 29–34
government documents as, 34–35
periodicals as, 24–28
reference works as, 16–24
square brackets, 56, 106, 152
subheadings, in APA manuscript style, 140
subject (of essay)
assessing, 61–62
of research paper, 7–9
summary, in notes, 58
superscript, 86, 94, 160
syllabication, 207–8

television program
endnote citation of, 172
MLA citation of, 54
theater, reference works for, 24
title
abbreviation of, 204–5
capitalization of, 199, 200
italics with, 206

title page
  APA format for, 133, 136
  MLA format for, 88, 95
translation
  APA citation of, 117
  endnote citation of, 165–66
  MLA citation of, 44

videotape
  APA citation of, 124–25

endnote citation of, 172
MLA citation of, 54

Wilsearch, 31–33
working bibliography, 37
  assembling, 38
  recording information in, 38–39
Works Cited page, 38, 78–87
  sample, 111